ARCHITECT REGISTRATION EXAM

# SITE PLANNING & DESIGN

## ARE SAMPLE PROBLEMS AND PRACTICE EXAM

SECOND EDITION

## DAVID KENT BALLAST, FAIA

**The Power to Pass**
www.ppi2pass.com

Professional Publications, Inc. • Belmont, California

# How to Locate and Report Errata for This Book

At PPI, we do our best to bring you error-free books. But when errors do occur, we want to make sure you can view corrections and report any potential errors you find, so the errors cause as little confusion as possible.

A current list of known errata and other updates for this book is available on the PPI website at **www.ppi2pass.com/errata**. We update the errata page as often as necessary, so check in regularly. You will also find instructions for submitting suspected errata. We are grateful to every reader who takes the time to help us improve the quality of our books by pointing out an error.

SITE PLANNING & DESIGN:
ARE SAMPLE PROBLEMS AND PRACTICE EXAM
**Second Edition**

Current printing of this edition: 1

**Printing History**

| edition number | printing number | update |
|---|---|---|
| 1 | 1 | New book. |
| 1 | 2 | Minor corrections. |
| 2 | 1 | Updated vignettes. |

Printed in the United States of America

PPI
1250 Fifth Avenue, Belmont, CA 94002
(650) 593-9119
www.ppi2pass.com

ISBN-13: 978-1-59126-154-4

# TABLE OF CONTENTS

# PREFACE AND ACKNOWLEDGMENTS

This book is tailored to the needs of those studying for version 4.0 of the Architect Registration Examination. The ARE 4.0 is one step in a process of change that began in 2001, when the National Council of Architectural Registration Boards (NCARB) published the results of a two-year study of the architecture profession. Since then, in response to that study, NCARB has introduced a series of changes to the ARE. Previous versions of the ARE have reduced the number of graphic vignettes and introduced new types of questions. Version 4.0, though, is the most substantial change yet, reorganizing and reducing the number of divisions and integrating graphic vignettes into divisions that were previously multiple choice only.

In the ARE 4.0, NCARB has eliminated the graphics-only Building Technology division and redistributed its six graphic vignettes into other divisions, combining them with multiple-choice sections of the exam. Each multiple-choice section carried over from version 3.1 now contains fewer questions, and a multiple-choice section has been added to the Site Planning & Design division (formerly called just Site Planning). The two structural divisions from version 3.1, General Structures and Lateral Forces, are now combined into one division, Structural Systems. In all, there are now seven divisions instead of nine, and there are somewhat fewer multiple-choice questions in all on the ARE 4.0 than on version 3.1.

In response to the version 4.0 changes, PPI has reorganized and revised its ARE review books. *ARE Review Manual* now covers all the divisions of the ARE in a single volume. This new book, *Site Planning & Design: ARE Sample Problems and Practice Exam*, is one of seven companion volumes, one for each ARE 4.0 division. We believe that this organization will help you study for individual divisions most effectively.

For the second edition, I have revised the two Site Grading vignettes to reflect a change made by NCARB in the ARE 4.0. In the ARE 3.1, you were given the location of a rectangular platform or other object to be built on a site, and were required to regrade the site appropriately. In the new version of this vignette, you must also choose a suitable location for the object before you regrade.

You will find that this book and the related volumes are valuable parts of your exam preparation. Although there is no substitute for a good formal education and the broad-based experience provided by your internship with a practicing architect, this review series will help direct your study efforts to increase your chances of passing the ARE.

Many people have helped in the production of this book. I would like to thank all the fine people at PPI including Scott Marley (project editor), Amy Schwertman (typesetter, cover designer, and illustrator), and Thomas Bergstrom (illustrator).

David Kent Ballast, FAIA

# INTRODUCTION

## ABOUT THIS BOOK

*Site Planning & Design: ARE Sample Problems and Practice Exam* is written to help you prepare for the Site Planning & Design division of the Architect Registration Examination (ARE), version 4.0.

Although this book can be a valuable study aid by itself, it is designed to be used along with the *ARE Review Manual*, also published by PPI. The *ARE Review Manual* is organized into sections that cover all seven divisions of the ARE 4.0.

- Programming, Planning & Practice
- Site Planning & Design
- Schematic Design
- Structural Systems
- Building Systems
- Building Design & Construction Systems
- Construction Documents & Services

This book is one of seven companion volumes to the *ARE Review Manual* that PPI publishes. Each of these books contains sample problems and practice exams for one of the ARE 4.0 divisions.

- *Programming, Planning & Practice: ARE Sample Problems and Practice Exam*
- *Site Planning & Design: ARE Sample Problems and Practice Exam*
- *Schematic Design: ARE Sample Problems and Practice Exam*
- *Structural Systems: ARE Sample Problems and Practice Exam*
- *Building Systems: ARE Sample Problems and Practice Exam*
- *Building Design & Construction Systems: ARE Sample Problems and Practice Exam*
- *Construction Documents & Services: ARE Sample Problems and Practice Exam*

## THE ARCHITECT REGISTRATION EXAMINATION

Congratulations on completing (or nearing the end of) the Intern Development Program! You are two-thirds of the way to being able to call yourself an architect. NAAB degree? Check. IDP? Check. Now on to step three.

The final hurdle is the Architect Registration Examination. The ARE is a uniform test administered to candidates who wish to become licensed architects after they have served their required internships. It is given in all fifty states, all ten Canadian provinces, and five other jurisdictions including the District of Columbia, Guam, the Northern Mariana Islands, Puerto Rico, and the Virgin Islands.

The ARE has been developed to protect the health, safety, and welfare of the public by testing a candidate's entry-level competence to practice architecture. Its content relates as closely as possible to situations encountered in practice. It tests for the kinds of knowledge, skills, and abilities required of an entry-level architect, with particular emphasis on those services that affect public health, safety, and welfare. In order to accomplish these objectives, the exam tests for

- knowledge in specific subject areas
- the ability to make decisions
- the ability to consolidate and use information to solve a problem
- the ability to coordinate the activities of others on the building team

The ARE also includes some professional practice and project management questions.

The ARE is developed jointly by the National Council of Architectural Registration Boards (NCARB) and the Committee of Canadian Architectural Councils (CCAC), with the assistance of the Chauncey Group International and Prometric. The Chauncey Group serves as NCARB's test development and operations consultant, and Prometric operates and maintains the test centers where the ARE is administered.

Although the responsibility of professional licensing rests with each individual state, every state's board requires successful completion of the ARE to achieve registration or licensure. One of the primary reasons for a uniform test is to facilitate reciprocity—that is, to enable an architect to more easily gain a license to practice in states other than the one in which he or she was originally licensed.

The ARE is administered and graded entirely by computer. All divisions of the exam are offered six days a week at a network of test centers across North America. The results are scored by computer, and the results are forwarded to individual state boards of architecture, which process them and send them to candidates. If you fail a division, you must wait six months before you can retake that division.

## First Steps

As you begin to prepare for the exam, you should first obtain a current copy of *ARE Guidelines* from NCARB. This booklet will get you started with the exam process and will be a valuable reference throughout. It includes descriptions of the seven divisions, instructions on how to apply, pay for, and take the ARE, and other useful information. You can download a PDF version at www.ncarb.org, or you can request a printed copy through the contact information provided at that site.

The NCARB website also gives current information about the exam, education requirements, training, examination procedures, and NCARB reciprocity services. It includes sample scenarios of the computer-based examination process and examples of costs associated with taking the computer-based exam.

The PPI website is also a good source of exam info (at **www.ppi2pass.com/areinfo**) and answers to frequently asked questions (at **www.ppi2pass.com/arefaq**).

To register as an examinee, you should obtain the registration requirements from the board in the state, province, or territory where you want to be registered. The exact requirements vary from one jurisdiction to another, so contact your local board. Links to state boards can be found at **www.ppi2pass.com/areinfo**.

As soon as NCARB has verified your qualifications and you have received your "Authorization to Test" letter, you may begin scheduling examinations. The exams are offered on a first come, first served basis and must be scheduled at least 72 hours in advance. See *ARE Guidelines* for instructions on finding a current list of testing centers. You may take the exams at any location, even outside the state in which you intend to become registered.

You may schedule any division of the ARE at any time and may take the divisions in any order. Divisions can be taken one at a time, to spread out preparation time and exam costs, or can be taken together in any combination.

However, each candidate must pass all seven divisions of the ARE within a single five-year period. This period, or "rolling clock," begins on the date of the first division you passed. If you have not completed the ARE within five years, the divisions that you passed more than five years ago are no longer credited, and the content in them must be retaken. Your new five-year period begins on the date of the earliest division you passed within the last five years.

## About the ARE 4.0

NCARB's introduction of ARE version 4.0 in July 2008 marked the change to an exam format with both multiple-choice and graphic subjects appearing within the same division. In the previous version, the ARE 3.1, each division contained either multiple-choice problems or graphic problems, never both.

The ARE 4.0 also has fewer divisions than the ARE 3.1, seven instead of nine. The organization of the ARE 4.0 exam means that candidates will make fewer trips to the test center, and can study for related portions of the exam all at once.

Some candidates who began taking the ARE 3.1 before the change will have to transition to the ARE 4.0. For information and advice, see **www.ppi2pass.com/aretransition**.

This book and its companion volumes are organized to help you study for the ARE 4.0. If you are studying for the ARE 3.1, you may prefer to study with the books in PPI's Architecture Exam Review series, which are organized for that version of the exam.

## Examination Format

The ARE 4.0 is organized into seven divisions that test various areas of architectural knowledge and problem-solving ability.

### Programming, Planning & Practice

    85 multiple-choice questions
    1 graphic vignette: Site Zoning

### Site Planning & Design

    65 multiple-choice questions
    2 graphic vignettes: Site Design, Site Grading

### Schematic Design

    2 graphic vignettes: Building Layout, Interior Layout

### Structural Systems

    125 multiple-choice questions
    1 graphic vignette: Structural Layout

**Building Systems**

95 multiple-choice questions
1 graphic vignette: Mechanical & Electrical Plan

**Building Design & Construction Systems**

85 multiple-choice questions
3 graphic vignettes: Accessibility/Ramp, Roof Plan, Stair Design

**Construction Documents & Services**

100 multiple-choice questions
1 graphic vignette: Building Section

Experienced test-takers will tell you that there is quite a bit of overlap among these divisions. Questions that seem better suited to the Construction Documents & Services division may show up on the Building Design & Construction Systems division, for example, and questions on architectural history and building regulations might show up anywhere. That's why it's important to have a comprehensive strategy for studying and taking the exams.

The ARE is given entirely by computer. There are two kinds of problems on the exam. Multiple-choice problems are short questions presented on the computer screen; you answer them by clicking on the right answer or answers, or by filling in a blank. Graphic vignettes are longer problems in design; you solve a vignette by planning and drawing your solution on the computer. Six of the seven divisions contain both multiple-choice sections and graphic vignettes; the Schematic Design division contains only vignettes. Both kinds of problems are described later in this Introduction.

## STUDY GUIDELINES

After the five to seven years (or even more) of higher education you've received to this point, you probably have a good idea of the study strategy that works best for you. The trick is figuring out how to apply that to the ARE. Unlike many college courses, there isn't a textbook or set of class notes from which all the exam questions will be derived. The exams are very broad and draw questions from multiple areas of knowledge.

The first challenge, then, is figuring out what to study. The ARE is never quite the same exam twice. The field of knowledge tested is always the same, but the specific questions asked are drawn randomly from a large pool, and will differ from one candidate to the next. One division may contains many code-related questions for one candidate and only a few for the next. This makes the ARE a challenge to study for.

*ARE Guidelines* contains lists of resources recommended by NCARB. That list can seem overwhelming, though, and on top of that, many of the recommended books are expensive or no longer in print. To help address this problem, a number of publishers sell study guides for the ARE. These guides summarize the information found in primary sources such as the NCARB-recommended books. A list of helpful resources for preparing for the Site Planning & Design division can also be found in the Recommended Reading section of this book.

Your method of studying for the ARE should be based on both the content and form of the exam and on your school and work experience. Because the exam covers such a broad range of subject matter, it cannot possibly include every detail of practice. Rather, it tends to focus on what is considered entry-level knowledge and knowledge that is important for the protection of the public's health, safety, and welfare. Other types of questions are asked, too, but this knowledge should be the focus of your review schedule.

Your recent work experience should also help you determine what areas to study the most. A candidate who has been involved with construction documents for several years will probably need less review in that area than in others he or she has not had recent experience with.

The *ARE Review Manual* and its companion volumes are structured to help candidates focus on the topics that are more likely to be included in the exam in one form or another. Some subjects may seem familiar or may be easy to recall from memory, and others may seem completely foreign; the latter are the ones to give particular attention to. It may be wise to study additional sources on these subjects, take review seminars, or get special help from someone who is knowledgeable in the topic.

A typical candidate might spend about forty hours preparing for and taking each exam. Some will need to study more, some less. Forty hours is about one week of studying eight hours a day, or two weeks of four hours a day, or a month of two hours a day, along with reasonable breaks and time to attend to other responsibilities. As you probably work full time and have other family and personal obligations, it is important to develop a realistic schedule and do your best to stick to it. The ARE is not the kind of exam you can cram for the night before.

Also, because the fees are high and retaking a test is expensive, you want to do your best and pass in as few tries as possible. Allowing enough time to study and going into each exam well prepared will help you relax and concentrate on the questions.

The following steps may provide a useful structure for an exam study program.

Step 1: Start early. You can't review for a test like this by starting two weeks before the date. This is especially true if you are taking all portions of the exam for the first time.

Step 2: Go through the *ARE Review Manual* quickly to get a feeling for the scope of the subject matter and how the major topics are organized. Whatever division you're studying for, plan to review the chapters on building regulations as well. Review *ARE Guidelines*.

Step 3: Based on your review of the *ARE Review Manual* and *ARE Guidelines*, and on a realistic appraisal of your strong and weak areas, set priorities for study and determine which topics need more study time.

Step 4: Divide review subjects into manageable units and organize them into a sequence of study. It is generally best to start with the less familiar subjects. Based on the exam date and plans for beginning study, assign a time limit to each study unit. Again, your knowledge of a subject should determine the time devoted to it. You may want to devote an entire week to earthquake design if it is an unfamiliar subject, and only one day to timber design if it is a familiar one. In setting up a schedule, be realistic about other life commitments as well as your personal ability to concentrate on studying over a length of time.

Step 5: Begin studying, and stick with the schedule. Of course, this is the most difficult part of the process and the one that requires the most self-discipline. The job should be easier if you have started early and if you are following a realistic schedule that allows time for recreation and personal commitments.

Step 6: Stop studying a day or two before the exam. Relax. By this time, no amount of additional cramming will help.

At some point in your studying, you will want to spend some time becoming familiar with the program you will be using to solve the graphic vignettes, which does not resemble commercial CAD software. The software and sample vignettes can be downloaded from the NCARB website at www.ncarb.org.

There are many schools of thought on the best order for taking the divisions. One factor to consider is the six-month waiting period before you can retake a particular division. It's never fun to predict what you might fail, but if you know that a specific area might give you trouble, consider taking that exam near the beginning. You might be pleasantly surprised when you check the mailbox, but if not, as you work through the rest of the exams, the clock will be ticking and you can schedule the retest six months later.

Here are some additional tips.

• Learn concepts first, and then details later. For example, it is much better to understand the basic ideas and theories of waterproofing than it is to attempt to memorize dozens of waterproofing products and details. Once the concept is clear, the details are much easier to learn and to apply during the exam.

• Use the index to the *ARE Review Manual* to focus on particular subjects in which you feel weak, especially subjects that can apply to more than one division.

• Don't tackle all your hardest subjects first. Make one of your early exams one that you feel fairly confident about. It's nice to get off on the right foot with a PASS.

• Programming, Planning & Practice and Building Design & Construction Systems both tend to be "catch-all" divisions that cover a lot of material from the Construction Documents & Services division as well as others. Consider taking Construction Documents & Services first among those three, and then the other two soon after.

• Many past candidates recommend taking the Programming, Planning & Practice division last or nearly last, so that you will be familiar with the body of knowledge for all the other divisions as well.

• Brush up on architectural history before taking any of the divisions with multiple-choice sections. Know major buildings and their architects, particularly structures that are representative of an architect's philosophy (for example, Le Corbusier and the Villa Savoye) or that represent "firsts" or "turning points."

• Try to schedule your exams so that you'll have enough time to get yourself ready, eat, and review a little. If you'll have a long drive to the testing center, try to avoid having to make it during rush hour.

• If you are planning to take more than one division at a time, do not overstudy any one portion of the exam. It is generally better to review the concepts than to try to become an overnight expert in one area. For example, the exam may ask general questions about plate girders, but it will not ask for a complete, detailed design of a plate girder.

- Solve as many sample problems as possible, including those provided with NCARB's practice program, the books of sample problems and practice exams published by PPI, and any others that are available.

- Take advantage of the community of intern architects going through this experience with you. Some local AIA chapters offer ARE preparation courses or may be able to help you organize a study group with other interns in your area. Visit website forums to discuss the exam with others who have taken it or are preparing to take it. The Architecture Exam Forum at **www.ppi2pass.com/areforum** is a great online resource for questions, study advice, and encouragement. Even though the ARE questions change daily, it is a good idea to get a feeling for the types of questions that are being asked, the general emphasis, and the subject areas that previous candidates have found particularly troublesome.

- A day or two before the first test session, stop studying in order to relax as much as possible. Get plenty of sleep the night before the test.

- Try to relax as much as possible during study periods and during the exam itself. Worrying is counterproductive. Candidates who have worked diligently in school, have obtained a wide range of experience during internship, and have started exam review early will be in the best possible position to pass the ARE.

## TAKING THE EXAM

### What to Bring

Bring multiple forms of photo ID and your Authorization to Test letter to the test site.

It is neither necessary nor permitted to bring any reference materials or scratch paper into the test site. Pencils and scratch paper are provided by the proctor and must be returned when leaving the exam room. Earplugs will also be provided. Leave all your books and notes in the car. Most testing centers have lockers for your keys, small personal belongings, and cell phone.

Do not bring a calculator into the test site. A calculator built into the testing software will be available in all divisions.

### Arriving at the Testing Center

Allow plenty of time to get to the exam site, to avoid transportation problems such as getting lost or stuck in traffic jams. If you can, arrive a little early, and take a little time in the parking lot to review one last time the formulas and other things you need to memorize. Then relax, take a few deep breaths, and go take the exam.

Once at the testing center, you will check in with the attendant, who will verify your identification and your Authorization to Test. (Don't forget to take this home with you after each exam; you'll need it for the next one.) After you check in, you'll be shown to your testing station.

When the exam begins, you will have the opportunity to click through a tutorial that explains how the computer program works. You'll probably want to read through it the first time, but after that initial exam, you will know how the software works and you won't need the tutorial. Take a deep breath, organize your paper and pencils, and take advantage of the opportunity to dump all the facts floating around in your brain onto your scratch paper—write down as much as you can. This includes formulas, ratios ("if $x$ increases, $y$ decreases"), and so on—anything that you are trying desperately not to forget. If you can get all the things you've crammed at the last minute onto that paper, you'll be able to think a little more clearly about the questions posed on the screen.

### Taking the Multiple-Choice Sections

The ARE multiple-choice sections include several types of questions.

One type of multiple-choice question is based on written, graphic, or photographic information. The candidate examines the information and selects the correct answer from four given answer choices. Some problems may require calculations.

A second type of multiple-choice question lists four or five items or statements, which are given Roman numerals from I to IV or I to V. For example, the question may give five statements about a subject, and the candidate must choose the statements that are true. The four answer choices are combinations of these numerals, such as "I and III" or "II, IV, and V".

A third type of multiple-choice question describes a situation that could be encountered in actual practice. Drawings, diagrams, photographs, forms, tables, or other data may also be given. The question asks the examinee to select the best answer from four options.

Two kinds of questions that NCARB calls "alternate item types" also show up in the multiple-choice sections. In a "fill in the blank" question, the examinee must fill a blank with a number derived from a table or calculation. In a "check all that apply" question, six answer choices are given, and the candidate must choose all the correct answers. The question tells how many of the choices are correct, from two to four.

The examinee must choose all the correct answers to receive credit; partial credit is not given.

Between 10% and 15% of the questions in a multiple-choice section will be these "alternate item type" questions. Every question on the ARE, however, counts the same toward your total score.

Keep in mind that multiple-choice questions often require the examinee to do more than just select an answer based on memory. At times it will be necessary to combine several facts, analyze data, perform a calculation, or review a drawing. Remember, too, that most candidates do not need the entire time allotted for the multiple-choice sections. If you have time for more than one pass through the questions, you can make good use of it.

Here are some tips for the multiple-choice problems.

- Go through the entire section in one somewhat swift pass, answering the questions that you're sure about and marking the others so you can return to them later. If a question requires calculations, skip it for now unless it's very simple. Then go back to the beginning and work your way through the exam again, taking a little more time to read each question and think through the answer.

- Another benefit of going through the entire section at the beginning is that occasionally there is information in one question that may help you answer another question somewhere else.

- If you are very unsure of a question, pick your best answer choice, mark it, and move on. You will probably have time at the end of the test to go back and recheck these answers. But remember, your first response is usually the best.

- Always answer all the questions. Unanswered questions are counted wrong, so even if you are just guessing, it's better to choose an answer and have a chance of it being correct than to skip it and be certain of getting it wrong. When faced with four answer choices, the old SAT strategy of eliminating the two answers that are definitely wrong and making your best guess between the two that remain is helpful on the ARE, too.

- Some questions may seem too simple. Although a few very easy and obvious questions are included on the ARE, more often the simplicity should serve as a red flag to warn you to reevaluate the question for exceptions to a rule or special circumstances that make the obvious, easy response incorrect.

- Watch out for absolute words in a question, such as "always," "never," and "completely." These are often a clue that some little exception exists, turning what reads like a true statement into a false one or vice versa.

- Be alert for words like "seldom," "usually," "best," and "most reasonable." These indicate that some judgment will be involved in answering the question. Look for two or more options that appear to be very similar.

- Some divisions will provide an on-screen reference sheet with useful formulas and other information that will help you solve some problems. Skim through the reference sheet so you know what information is there, and then use it as a resource.

- Occasionally there may be a defective question. This does not happen very often, but if it does, make the best choice possible under the circumstances. Flawed questions are usually discovered, and either they are not counted on the test or any one of the correct answers is credited.

## Solving the Vignettes

Each of the eleven graphic vignettes on the ARE is designed to test a particular area of knowledge and skill. Each one presents a base plan of some kind and gives programmatic and other requirements. The candidate must create a plan that satisfies the requirements.

The Site Design vignette requires the candidate to prepare a schematic site plan in response to various programmatic, functional, orientation, and setback requirements. The candidate must place buildings, accommodate both pedestrian and vehicular circulation, plan parking spaces, respond to climatic influences, and consider land use, views, and other requirements.

The Site Grading vignette tests the candidate's ability to manipulate site topography. The problem presents a site plan with contours, and a program. The candidate must manipulate the contour lines on the site to satisfy certain requirements.

The computer scores the vignettes by a complex grading method. Design criteria are given various point values, and responses are categorized as Acceptable, Unacceptable, or Indeterminate.

## General Tips for the Vignettes

Here are some general tips for approaching the vignettes. More detailed solving tips can be found in the solutions to each vignette.

- Remember that with the current format and computer grading, each vignette covers only a very specific area of knowledge and offers a limited number of possible solutions. In a few cases only one solution is really possible. Use this as an advantage.

- Read the problem thoroughly, twice. Follow the requirements exactly, letting each problem solve itself as much as possible. Be careful not to read more into the problem than is there. The test writers are very specific about what they want; there is no need to add to the problem requirements. If a particular type of solution is strongly suggested, follow that lead.

- Consider only those code requirements given in the vignette, even if they deviate from familiar codes. Do not read anything more into the problem. The code requirements may be slightly different from what candidates use in practice.

- Use the scratch paper provided to sketch possible solutions before starting the final solution.

- Make sure all programmed elements are included in the final design.

- When the functional requirements of the problem have been solved, use the problem statement as a checklist to make sure all criteria have been satisfied.

### General Tips for Using the Vignette Software

It is important to practice with the vignette software that will be used in the exam. The program is unique to the ARE and unlike standard CAD software. If you are unfamiliar with the software interface you will waste valuable time learning to use it, and are likely to run out of time before completing the vignettes. Practice software can be downloaded at no charge from NCARB's website at www.ncarb.org. Usage time for the practice program can also be purchased at Prometric test centers. The practice software includes tutorials, directions, and one practice vignette for each of the eleven vignettes.

Here are some general tips for using the vignette software.

- When elements overlap on the screen, it may be difficult to select a particular element. If this happens, repeatedly click on the element without moving the mouse until the desire element is highlighted.

- Try to stay in "ortho" mode. This mode can be used to solve most problems, and it makes the solution process much easier and quicker. Unless obviously required by the vignette, creating additional angles complicates any problem with the time restrictions given.

- If the vignette relates to contour modifications, it may help to draw schematic sections through the significant existing slopes. This provides a three-dimensional image of the problem.

- When drawing, if the program states that elements should connect, make sure they touch at their boundaries only and do not overlap. Use the *check* tool to determine if there are any overlaps. Walls that do not align correctly can cause a solution to be downgraded or even rejected. Remember, walls between spaces change color temporarily when properly aligned.

- Make liberal use of the *zoom* tool for sizing and aligning components accurately. Zoom in as closely as possible on the area being worked. When aligning objects, it is also helpful to use the full-screen cursor.

- Turn on the grid and verify spacing. This makes it easier to align objects and get a sense of the sizes of objects and the distances between them. Use the *measure* tool to check exact measurements if needed.

- Make liberal use of the sketch tools. These can be turned on and off and do not count during the grading, but they can be used to show relationships and for temporary guidelines and other notations.

- Use sketch circles to show required distances, setbacks, clearances, and similar measures.

## AFTER THE EXAM

When you've clicked the button to end the test, the computer may prompt you to provide some demographic information about yourself and your education and experience. Then gather your belongings, turn in your scratch paper and materials—you must leave them with the proctor—and leave the testing center. (For security reasons, you can't remove anything from the test center.) If the staff has retained your Authorization to Test and your identification, don't forget to retrieve both.

If you should encounter any problems during the exams or have any concerns, be sure to report them to the test center administrator and to NCARB as soon as possible. If you wait longer than ten days after you test, NCARB will not respond to your complaint. You must report your complaint immediately and directly to NCARB and copy your state registration board for any hope of assistance.

Then it's all over but the wait for the mail. How long it takes to get your scores will vary with the efficiency of your state registration board, which reviews the scores from NCARB before passing along the results. But four to six weeks is typical.

As you may have heard from classmates and colleagues, the ARE is a difficult exam—but it is certainly not impossible to pass. A solid architectural education and a well-rounded internship are the best preparation you can have. Watch carefully and listen to the vocabulary used by architects with more experience. Look for opportunities to participate in all phases of project delivery so that you have some "real world" experience to apply to the scenarios you will inevitably find in exam questions.

One last piece of advice is not to put off taking the exams. Take them as soon as you become eligible. You will probably still remember a little bit from your college courses and you may even have your old textbooks and notes handy. As life gets more complicated—with spouses and children and work obligations—it is easy to make excuses and never find time to get around to it. Make the commitment, and do it now. After all, this is the last step to reaching your goal of calling yourself an architect.

# HOW TO USE THIS BOOK

This book contains 61 sample multiple-choice problems and two sample vignettes, as well as one complete practice exam consisting of 65 multiple-choice problems and two vignettes. These have been written to help you prepare for the Site Planning & Design division of the Architect Registration Examination, version 4.0.

One of the best ways to prepare for the ARE is by solving sample problems. While you are studying for this division, use the sample problems in this book to make yourself familiar with the different types of questions and the breadth of topics you are likely to encounter on the actual exam. Then when it's time to take the ARE, you will already be comfortable with the format of the exam questions. Also, seeing which sample problems you can and cannot answer correctly will help you gauge your understanding of the topics covered in the Site Planning & Design division.

The sample multiple-choice problems in this book are organized by subject area, so that you can concentrate on one subject at a time if you like. Each problem is immediately followed by its answer and an explanation.

The sample vignette in this book can be solved directly on the base plan provided or on a sheet of tracing paper. Alternatively, you can download an electronic file of the base plan in PDF format from **www.ppi2pass.com/vignettes** for use in your own CAD program. (On the actual exam, vignettes are solved on the computer using NCARB's own software; see the Introduction for more information about this.) When you are finished with your solution to the vignette, compare it against the sample passing and failing solutions that follow. Individual target times are given for the vignettes in the Sample Problems section of this book, to give you an idea of how much time to budget for each one. On the actual exam (as in this book's practice exam), you will have a single period of time within which you must complete both vignettes.

While the sample problems in this book are intended for you to use as you study for the exam, the practice exam is best used only when you have almost finished your study of the Site Planning & Design topics. A week or two before you are scheduled to take the division, when you feel you are nearly ready for the exam, do a "dry run" by taking the practice exam in this book. This will hone your test-taking skills and give you a reality check about how prepared you really are.

The experience will be most valuable to you if you treat the practice exam as though it were an actual exam. Do not read the questions ahead of time and do not look at the solutions until after you've finished. Try to simulate the exam experience as closely as possible. This means locking yourself away in a quiet space, setting an alarm for the exam's testing time, and working through the entire examination with no coffee, television, or telephone—only your calculator, a pencil, your drafting tools or CAD program for the vignette, and a few sheets of scratch paper. (On the actual exam, these are provided.) This will help you prepare to budget your time, give you an idea of what the actual exam experience will be like, and help you develop a test-taking strategy that works for you.

The target times for the sections of the practice exam are

**Multiple choice:** 1.5 hours

**Vignettes:** 2 hours

Within the time allotted for each section, you may work on the questions or vignettes in any order and spend any amount of time on each one.

Record your answers for the multiple-choice section of the practice exam using the "bubble" answer form at the front of the exam. When you are finished, you can check your answers quickly against the filled-in answer key at the front of the Solutions section. Then turn to the solutions and read the explanations of the answers, especially those you answered incorrectly. The explanation will give you a better understanding of the intent of the question and why individual choices are right or wrong.

The Solutions section may also be used as a guide for the final phase of your studies. As opposed to a traditional study guide that is organized into chapters and paragraphs of facts, this question-and-answer format can help you see how the exam might address a topic, and what types of questions you are likely to encounter. If you still are not clear about a particular subject after reading a solution's explanation, review the subject in one of your study resources. Give yourself time for further study, and then take the multiple-choice section again.

The vignette portion of the practice exam can be solved the same way as the sample vignette, either directly on the base plans, on tracing paper, or with a CAD program using the electronic files downloaded from **www.ppi2pass.com/vignettes**. Try to solve both vignettes within the target time given. When you are finished, compare your drawings against the passing and failing solutions given in the Solutions section.

This book is best used in conjunction with your primary study source or study guide, such as PPI's *ARE Review Manual*. *Site Planning & Design: ARE Sample Problems and Practice Exam* is not intended to give you all the information you will need to pass this division of the ARE. Rather, it is designed to expose you to a variety of problem types and to help you sharpen your problem-solving and test-taking skills. With a sound review and the practice you'll get from this book, you'll be well on your way to successfully passing the Site Planning & Design division of the Architect Registration Examination.

# HOW SI UNITS ARE USED
# IN THIS BOOK

This book includes equivalent measurements in the text and illustrations using the Système International (SI), or the metric system as it is commonly called. However, the use of SI units for construction and book publishing in the United States is problematic. This is because the building construction industry in the United States (with the exception of federal construction) has generally not adopted the metric system. As a result, equivalent measurements of customary U.S. units (also called English or inch-pound units) are usually given as a *soft* conversion, in which customary U.S. measurements are simply converted into SI units using standard conversion factors. This always results in a number with excessive significant digits. When construction is done using SI units, the building is designed and drawn according to *hard* conversions, where planning dimensions and building products are based on a metric module from the beginning. For example, studs are spaced 400 mm on center to accommodate panel products that are manufactured in standard 1200 mm widths.

During the present time of transition to the Système International in the United States, code-writing bodies, federal laws such as the ADA, product manufacturers, trade associations, and other construction-related industries typically still use the customary U.S. system and make soft conversions to develop SI equivalents. In the case of some product manufacturers, they produce the same product using both measuring systems. Although there are industry standards for developing SI equivalents, there is no perfect consistency for rounding off when conversions are made. For example, the International Building Code shows a 152 mm equivalent when a 6 in dimension is required, while the Americans with Disabilities Act Accessibility Guidelines (ADAAG) give a 150 mm equivalent for the same customary U.S. dimension.

To further complicate matters, each book publisher may employ a slightly different house style in handling SI equivalents when customary U.S. units are used as the primary measuring system. The confusion is likely to continue until the United States construction industry adopts the SI system completely, eliminating the need for dual dimensioning in publishing.

For the purposes of this book, the following conventions have been adopted.

Throughout the book, the customary U.S. measurements are given first with the SI equivalent shown in parentheses. When the measurement is millimeters, units are not shown. For example, a dimension may be indicated as 4 ft 8 in (1422). When the SI equivalent is some other unit, such as for volume or area, the units are indicated. For example, 250 ft² (23 m²).

Following standard conventions, all SI distance measurements in illustrations are in millimeters unless specifically indicated as meters.

When a measurement is given as part of a problem scenario, the SI measurement is not necessarily meant to be roughly equal to the U.S. measurement. For example, a hypothetical force on a beam might be given as 12 kips (12 kN). 12 kips is actually equal to about 53.38 kN, but the intention in such cases is only to provide two problems, one in U.S. units and one in SI units, of about the same difficulty.

When dimensions are for informational use, the SI equivalent rounded to the nearest millimeter is used.

When dimensions are given and they relate to planning or design guidelines, the SI equivalent is rounded to the nearest 5 mm for numbers over a few inches and to the nearest 10 mm for numbers over a few feet. When the dimension exceeds several feet, the number is rounded to the nearest 100 mm. For example, if you need a space about 10 ft wide for a given activity, the modular, rounded SI equivalent will be given as 3000 mm. More exact conversions are not required.

When an item is only manufactured to a customary U.S. measurement, the nearest SI equivalent rounded to the nearest millimeter is given, unless the dimension is very small (as for metal gages), in which case a more precise decimal equivalent will be given. Some materials, such as glass, are often manufactured to SI sizes. So, for example, a nominal $\frac{1}{2}$ in thick piece of glass will have an SI equivalent of 13 mm but can be ordered as 12 mm.

When there is a hard conversion in the industry and an SI equivalent item is manufactured, the hard conversion is given. For example, a 24 × 24 ceiling tile would have the hard conversion of 600 × 600 (instead of 610) because these are manufactured and available in the United States.

When an SI conversion is used by a code agency, such as the International Building Code (IBC), or published in another regulation, such as the ADA Accessibility Guidelines, the SI equivalents used by the issuing agency are printed in this book. For example, the same 10 ft dimension given previously as 3000 mm for a planning guideline would have an SI equivalent of 3048 mm in the context of the IBC because this is what that code requires. The ADA Accessibility Guidelines generally follow the rounding rule, to take SI dimensions to the nearest 10 mm. For example, a 10 ft requirement for accessibility will be shown as 3050 mm. The code requirements for readers outside the United States may be slightly different.

This book uses different abbreviations for pounds of force and pounds of mass in customary U.S. units. The abbreviation used for pounds of force (pounds-force) is lbf, and the abbreviation used for pounds of mass (pounds-mass) is lbm.

# CODES AND STANDARDS USED IN THIS BOOK

Americans with Disabilities Act (ADA) and Architectural Barriers Act (ABA) Accessibility Guidelines, 2004.

International Code Council. *International Building Code*, 2006. Washington, DC.

U.S. Green Building Council. Leadership in Energy and Environmental Design (LEED®) 2009 Green Building Rating System for New Construction. Washington, DC.

# RECOMMENDED READING

## General Reference

Access Board. *ADAAG Manual: A Guide to the Americans with Disabilities Accessibility Guidelines*. East Providence, RI: BNI Building News.

————. *ADAAG Manual: Americans with Disabilities Act Accessibility Guidelines for Buildings and Facilities*. Washington, DC: U.S. Architectural and Transportation Barriers Compliance Board. www.access-board.gov/adaag/html/adaag.htm.

ARCOM. *MASTERSPEC*. Salt Lake City: ARCOM. (Familiarity with the format and language of specifications is very helpful.)

ARCOM and American Institute of Architects. *The Graphic Standards Guide to Architectural Finishes: Using Masterspec® to Evaluate, Select, and Specify Materials*. New York: John Wiley & Sons.

Ballast, David Kent, and Steven O'Hara. *ARE Review Manual*. Belmont, CA: PPI.

Canadian Commission on Building and Fire Codes. *National Building Code of Canada*. Ottawa: National Research Council of Canada.

Fitch, James Marston. *Historic Preservation: Curatorial Management of the Built World*. Charlottesville: University Press of Virginia.

Guthrie, Pat. *Architect's Portable Handbook*. New York: McGraw-Hill.

Harris, Cyril M., ed. *Dictionary of Architecture and Construction*. New York: McGraw-Hill.

International Code Council. *International Building Code*. Washington, DC: International Code Council.

————. *Standard on Accessible and Usable Buildings and Facilities* (ICC/ANSI A117.1). Washington, DC: American National Standards Institute, International Code Council.

Patterson, Terry L. *Illustrated 2000 Building Code Handbook*. New York: McGraw-Hill.

Ramsey, Charles G., and Harold R. Sleeper. *Architectural Graphic Standards*. New York: John Wiley & Sons. (The student edition is an acceptable substitute for the professional version.)

U.S. Green Building Council. *LEED Reference Package for New Construction and Major Renovations*. Washington, DC: U.S. Green Building Council.

## Site Planning & Design

Ambrose, James. *Subsurface Conditions*. Washington, DC: National Council of Architectural Registration Boards.

Ambrose, James, and Peter Brandow. *Simplified Site Design*. New York: John Wiley & Sons.

Beall, Christine, and Deborah Slaton. *Guide to Preparing Design and Construction Documents for Historic Projects* (TD-2-8). Alexandria, VA: Construction Specifications Institute and Association for Preservation Technology International.

Brown, G. Z., and Mark DeKay. *Sun, Wind, and Light*. New York: John Wiley & Sons.

Demkin, Joseph A., ed. *Architect's Handbook of Professional Practice* by the American Institute of Architects. New York: John Wiley & Sons. (The student edition is an acceptable substitute for the professional version.)

Givoni, Baruch. Climate *Considerations in Building and Urban Design*. New York: John Wiley & Sons.

Katz, Peter. *The New Urbanism: Toward an Architecture of Community*. New York: McGraw-Hill.

Kostof, Spiro. *A History of Architecture: Settings and Rituals*. New York: Oxford University Press.

Kostof, Spiro, and Richard Tobias. *The City Assembled: The Elements of Urban Form Through History*. Boston, MA: Bulfinch Press.

Kumlin, Robert R. *Architectural Programming: Creative Techniques for Design Professionals*. New York: McGraw-Hill, Inc.

Lynch, Kevin. *The Image of the City*. Cambridge, MA: MIT Press.

Lynch, Kevin, and Gary Hack. *Site Planning*. Cambridge, MA: MIT Press.

McHarg, Ian L. *Design with Nature*. New York: John Wiley & Sons.

Newman, Oscar. *Creating Defensible Space*. Washington, DC: U.S. Department of Housing and Urban Development.

Olgyay, Victor. *Design with Climate*. New York: Van Nostrand Reinhold.

Parker, Harry, John W. MacGuire, and James Ambrose. *Simplified Site Engineering*. New York: John Wiley & Sons.

Peña, William, *and Steven A. Parshall. Problem Seeking: An Architectural Programming Primer*. New York: John Wiley & Sons.

U.S. Department of Energy and Public Technology, Inc. *Sustainable Building Technical Manual: Green Building Design, Construction, and Operations*. Washington, DC: Public Technology, Inc.

## Graphic Vignettes

Allen, Edward, and Joseph Iano. *The Architect's Studio Companion: Rules of Thumb for Preliminary Design*. New York: John Wiley & Sons.

Ambrose, James, and Peter Brandow. *Simplified Site Design*. New York: John Wiley & Sons.

Ching, Francis D. K., and Steven R. Winkel. *Building Codes Illustrated: A Guide to Understanding the International Building Code*. New York: John Wiley & Sons.

Hoke, John Ray, ed. *Architectural Graphic Standards*. New York: John Wiley & Sons.

Karlen, Mark. *Space Planning Basics*. New York: John Wiley & Sons.

Parker, Harry, John W. MacGuire, and James Ambrose. *Simplified Site Engineering*. New York: John Wiley & Sons.

## Architectural History

(Brush up on this before taking any of the multiple-choice exams, as architectural history questions are scattered throughout the sections.)

Curtis, William J.R. *Modern Architecture Since 1900*. London: Phaedon Press, Ltd.

Frampton, Kenneth. *Modern Architecture: A Critical History*. London: Thames and Hudson.

Trachtenberg, Marvin, and Isabelle Hyman. *Architecture: From Pre-History to Post-Modernism*. Englewood Cliffs, NJ: Prentice-Hall.

# SAMPLE PROBLEMS

## SITE ANALYSIS

1.  What is especially important in designing roads for drainage?

    A.  curbs and gutters
    B.  crown
    C.  catch basin
    D.  superelevation

### Solution

All roads should have a *crown*, or high point, in the center to ensure positive drainage to either side.

**The answer is B.**


2.  Wastewater flows because of differences in elevation

    A.  between catch basin entrances
    B.  between storm sewer vents
    C.  between drain inlets
    D.  along inverts

### Solution

The difference in elevation between two points at the bottom, or invert, of a sewer line is what causes the water flow. The term *invert* is also used to call out the bottom of drains, catch basins, and manholes.

**The answer is D.**


3.  Which of the following statements is INCORRECT?

    A.  A $1^1/_2$% slope is suitable for rough paving.
    B.  Landscaped areas near buildings should have at least a 2% slope away from the structure.
    C.  A safe sidewalk slopes no more than $2^1/_2$%.
    D.  Roads in northern climates can safely have up to a 12% grade.

### Solution

Most roads should be kept at a grade of less than 10%; very short roads and parking garage ramps are exceptions. In northern climates, where snow and ice are a problem, it is even more important to maintain gentle slopes. A 12% grade would not be safe and could make driving difficult. Table 2.1 in *ARE Review Manual* lists recommended slopes for various uses.

**The answer is D.**


4.  A soil investigation for a building site reveals that the soil type is sandy clay and that bentonite is present. Which of the following foundation types would be most appropriate?

    A.  spread footings
    B.  mat foundation
    C.  belled piers
    D.  grade beam on piers

### Solution

Grade beams on piers are used where expansive soil such as bentonite is present. The beams transfer the building weight to the piers, which are commonly placed on bedrock. Voids under the beams allow the soil to expand without heaving the foundation.

Each soil type has a certain bearing capacity, which is the load (measured in pounds per square foot or kilopascals) from a building foundation that the soil can resist. Of the various soil types, bedrock and sedimentary rock have the highest bearing capacities.

**The answer is D.**

5.    Four possible locations for a one-story building on a given site are shown, along with the site contours.

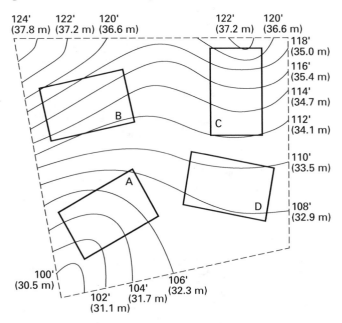

Which of the locations would require the LEAST expensive regrading?

    A.    location A
    B.    location B
    C.    location C
    D.    location D

### Solution

There are two considerations in this question: the amount of grading required to provide a level pad for the building, and the grading required to establish good drainage away from the building. Because location D is on the shallowest portion of the site, it would require the least cut-and-fill work to provide a level site, and drainage could easily be accomplished.

Since site A is in a valley (i.e., it is a drainage swale), it would be difficult to resolve the drainage problems here. Site B is on a steep slope and would need extensive cut-and-fill work to provide a level pad. Since site C is on a ridge, severe cutting would be required to level the site, although drainage would be easily accomplished.

*Study Note:* This is a common type of question designed to test knowledge and understanding of how topography affects site selection and building planning. You may be given a single site with a topography and asked to select the best location for a given use, or may be given four different topographic layouts and asked which is best suited for a particular project. The question may focus on how topography affects the cost of moving earth, drainage, solar access, road planning, aesthetics, or some combination of these.

**The answer is D.**

6.    What is the maximum slope on which it is feasible to plant grass?

    A.    5%
    B.    10%
    C.    15%
    D.    25%

### Solution

Grass in recreational areas should be limited to a 3% maximum slope, but grass for landscaping can be planted on slopes up to 25%. Slopes greater than 25% are difficult to mow and another ground cover should be used for them.

**The answer is D.**

7.    How does a retention pond manage stormwater runoff?

    A.    by slowing it and allowing sediments to settle while letting the water seep into the ground
    B.    by holding the excess until it can discharge at a controlled rate into the storm sewer system
    C.    by preventing it from contaminating other portions of the site
    D.    by retaining it until it can seep into the ground

### Solution

A *retention pond*, also called a holding pond or catch basin, prevents excessive stormwater runoff on a site from overloading the storm sewer system by temporarily holding the water and releasing it at a controlled rate.

Construction that is designed to allow sediment to settle while water drains into the ground is called a *bioswale*. Construction designed to retain stormwater until it can seep into the ground is called an *infiltration basin*.

*Study note:* The term *catch basin* sometimes also refers to a storm drainage structure that is designed to collect grit and trash while allowing the stormwater to flow out the drainage pipes.

**The answer is B.**

8.     What is the recommended maximum slope for a paved parking area?

     A.  1%

     B.  3%

     C.  5%

     D.  10%

*Solution*

The recommended maximum slope for a parking lot is 5%, although some sources suggest 6%. The maximum slope for an accessible portion of the parking area (according to the ADA-ABA Accessibility Guidelines) is 2%. The required minimum slope for drainage is 1.5%, though a 2% minimum slope is recommended.

*Study note:* A 12% slope is considered the maximum for automobile ramps where pedestrians are allowed, while a 15% slope is the maximum for automobile ramps where pedestrians are prohibited.

**The answer is C.**

9.     On a site with extensive development of buildings, roads, and parking, which change in drainage would have the most significant negative impact?

     A.  a decrease in pervious paving

     B.  an increase in water held on site

     C.  an increase in the number of drainage grates

     D.  an increase in the overall runoff coefficient

*Solution*

The *runoff coefficient* is the fraction of total precipitation falling on a surface that runs off the surface or is not absorbed into the ground. Although the runoff coefficients may vary slightly depending on the types of paving materials used, on a site with a great deal of hard-surface development, more stormwater would have to be diverted to a storm drainage system or to natural waterways. It is preferable to minimize the amount of water allowed to run off a site.

From the information given in the problem statement, it is not clear whether or not pervious paving would be used. With a large amount of hard-surface development, the amount of water held on site would decrease, rather than increase. The number of drainage grates would most likely increase, but this is not the most significant problem.

*Study note:* The runoff coefficient is used to calculate the amount of runoff in cubic feet (meters) per second on a site. The calculation takes into account the rainfall intensity and the area of the site. The runoff coefficient value ranges from almost zero for wooded areas with spongy soil to 1.0 for totally waterproof surfaces. The formula is $Q = CIA$, where $C$ is the runoff coefficient, $I$ is the rainfall intensity in inches per hour (meters per second) and $A$ is the area of the surface in acres (hectares).

**The answer is D.**

10.    Reinforced concrete or masonry retaining walls are usually necessary when

     A.  the height of the wall exceeds 4 ft (1220)

     B.  expansive clay soil is present

     C.  the groundwater level is above the lowest exposed portion of the wall

     D.  drainage behind the retaining wall is a problem

*Solution*

Retaining walls less than 4 ft (1220) high can usually be constructed of any suitable material, such as stones, loose-laid blocks, or preservative-treated wood. Higher walls become subject to sliding and overturning forces and must be engineered to resist the expected loads. Typically these engineered retaining walls are constructed of concrete or masonry and are built on footings.

The type of soil, the groundwater level, and the soil porosity alone do not dictate the use of reinforced concrete or masonry.

**The answer is A.**

11.    Information about the elevations or contours of a building site is found in a

     A.  deed of trust

     B.  metes and bounds description

     C.  plat

     D.  survey

*Solution*

Of the choices given, a *survey* is the only document that includes information on land elevations, which are indicated either with spot elevations or continuous contours.

A *deed of trust* is a written document that primarily describes the owner of the property and from whom it was purchased. A deed includes a description of the property, either by address or lot description, but does not include land elevation information. A *metes and bounds* description is a written description of the boundaries of a parcel of land. It defines the perimeter of the site by using a starting point and describing each boundary line by angle of bearing and length. A *plat* is a legal description of a subdivided piece of property that includes information on lots, streets, rights-of-way, and easements, among other items.

**The answer is D.**

12.  Information about street drainage in a city would be obtained by contacting the city's

     A.  public works department
     B.  building department
     C.  planning department
     D.  department of highways

*Solution*

The public works department (or a similarly named department) would be responsible for design and maintenance of a city's road drainage, which would be part of the storm sewage system.

The department of highways would most likely be the state agency responsible for design and construction of the roads themselves. Building departments and planning departments are not directly involved in wastewater drainage.

**The answer is A.**

13.  Information on the bearing capacity of soil is obtained from the

     A.  city engineer
     B.  general contractor
     C.  structural engineer
     D.  geotechnical consultant

*Solution*

The geotechnical consultant, or soils engineer, performs tests on site and in the laboratory to determine, among other things, the bearing capacity of the soil. The consultant

may then recommend the best type of foundation system for the soil conditions.

**The answer is D.**

# URBAN DEVELOPMENT AND COMMUNITY INFLUENCES

14.  In order to strengthen the sense of neighborhood and community, a developer constructs a public square in the middle of a housing development. The public square is an example of

     A.  a landmark
     B.  an edge
     C.  a district
     D.  a node

*Solution*

A *node* is a center of interest that people can enter, such as a plaza, a public square, or the intersection of paths. A node is smaller than a district and may be the center of a district.

A *landmark* is a point reference and a device for wayfinding and symbolic identification of an area. A *district* is a two-dimensional area that people perceive as having a common, identifying character and that is critical to the sense of neighborhood. An *edge* is a linear element other than a path that forms a boundary between two districts or that breaks continuity.

     *Study Note:* This question requires an understanding of the ideas of Kevin Lynch as described in his book, *The Image of the City*.

**The answer is D.**

15.  Several sites are being considered for the construction of a new community college. The most appropriate site would be the one adjacent to

     A.  two major intersecting highways
     B.  libraries and shopping
     C.  a technology-oriented office campus
     D.  a residential neighborhood and public transportation

*Solution*

A community college is a regional resource and would benefit from easy access to transportation sources encompassing a wide area, which two highways would provide.

Option D is not correct because, although public transportation is also a requirement, a large-scale development like a community college would not be appropriate for a residential neighborhood.

*Study Note:* This question requires an understanding of whether the proposed land use is local, district, or regional in nature and what the compatible uses are. A locally based project, such as a branch library or church, is compatible with residential uses and pedestrian transportation, while regionally based projects require public or vehicular transportation.

**The answer is A.**

16. The construction of a large general hospital is being planned for a neighborhood that lies between an outer edge of a downtown area and a medium- to high-density housing area. There are already smaller clinics and doctors' offices in the area. The following concerns have been addressed in the design of the hospital building. In presenting the project to the city planning board, which concern should the architect emphasize?

  A. The proposed street closure, planned in order to expand the building site, will not affect traffic.
  B. Sufficient parking will be made available on the project site.
  C. The bulk of the building design will not block sunlight from the housing.
  D. Sewer and water services will not have to be expanded to serve the building.

*Solution*

All these issues are important, but the architect wants to tailor the presentation toward the key concerns of the planning board and the community at large. In this type of neighborhood, parking would already be in short supply considering the number of downtown workers, housing, and the high-traffic needs of clinics and doctors' offices. Therefore, parking would likely be the most important concern to the community.

*Study Note:* This question and others like it require an understanding of all the major elements of planning a project and their effect on transportation services, traffic, utilities, ecology, drainage, and aesthetics. The examinee may also be asked questions about what types of drawings or other documentation could best show a proposed project in its neighborhood context. In general, know how the surroundings affect the project and how the project affects the surrounding community. Questions and answer choices are often ambiguous and require the examinee to make fine distinctions between possible answers.

*Terms to Know*

*catchment area:* the area surrounding a land development site, encompassing the population base that the development is meant to serve

*contextualism:* the belief that new buildings should be designed to harmonize with other buildings and elements in the vicinity

*demographics:* the statistical data of a population, such as age, income, and so forth

*personal space* (also called *personal distance*): the subjective distance or area surrounding a person's body into which a person feels comfortable allowing others to intrude, depending on the situation. Psychologist Robert Sommer developed a theory that there are four distances of personal space, including intimate distance, personal distance, social distance, and public distance—all of which vary by culture and specific situation.

*planned unit development (PUD):* a large parcel of land, typically with a mix of uses, that has been designed and laid out according to principles approved by the local planning authority and often with citizen input. A PUD is commonly used to develop land in a way that ordinarily would not be allowed based on normal planning and zoning restrictions of a jurisdiction.

*proxemics:* a term coined by anthropologist Edward T. Hall and now used to describe the study of the spatial requirements of humans and the effects of population density on behavior, communication, and social interaction

*superblock:* a large parcel of land designed to minimize the impact of the automobile on residential development in which access to interior lots is provided by cul-de-sacs branching from surrounding streets and providing one or more open spaces

*tax base:* the object on which a tax is calculated. For example, property is the tax base of a property tax.

**The answer is B.**

17. Which of the following design features would have the most detrimental effect on the environment of the surrounding neighborhood in an urban setting?

  A. square building shape
  B. dark exterior colors
  C. extensive exterior paving
  D. reflective glass

## Solution

Reflective glass would subject the surrounding buildings, streets, and pedestrian areas to harsh reflective light and heat during most of the day. Moreover, it would affect the surrounding areas throughout the day and during all times of the year.

A square building shape would not have much of an effect other than to cast a shadow during the day. Dark colors would generally absorb heat and affect the building itself more than the surrounding environment or microclimate. Extensive exterior paving would tend to absorb heat and affect the microclimate, but primarily in the immediate area of the paving.

**The answer is D.**

18.    In a dense urban context, site analysis prior to design should include studies of which of the following? (Choose the four that apply.)

    A.   solar shading
    B.   drainage
    C.   imageability
    D.   surrounding historical context
    E.   land values
    F.   views

## Solution

A *solar shading* study would show how the proposed building would block sunlight on other buildings as well as on the streets and outdoor areas. An *imageability* study determines how existing buildings, streets, and public spaces contribute to the neighborhood's image; that is, those elements defined by Kevin Lynch in his book, *The Image of the City*. This information could then be used to suggest ways that the proposed building could reinforce the existing urban context.

A study of the neighborhood's historic context would reveal significant historic structures and influences and may suggest how the proposed building could better fit into the community. A *view analysis* would show the significant views from the site and indicate where windows, entries, and how other features on the proposed building should be positioned.

In a dense urban area, drainage would not be an important consideration for early site analysis, as most of the site would be taken up with buildings. Land values would have already had an effect on the decision to purchase the site and is not critical for site analysis prior to design.

**The answer is A, C, D, and F.**

19.    With regard to the theories of proxemics, which approach to the design of a plaza would probably accommodate the most people while allowing individuals to maintain comfortable personal space distances?

    A.   a large, flat, open space with trees defining the perimeter
    B.   a heavily landscaped area with areas of lawn
    C.   an amphitheater with bench-type seating in raised tiers
    D.   a space with various levels, benches, and spaces defined by low walls

## Solution

*Proxemics* is a term used by Edward T. Hall for his theory of cultural use of space. Proxemics deals with issues of territoriality, spacing and positioning between people, and how the organization of the environment can affect these issues.

When designing a plaza that could accommodate a large number of closely spaced people, the designer may incorporate features that provide a sense of territoriality, encourage actual or imagined separation, and offer a choice of varying spatial positions. These elements could be provided by using design features such as changes of level; juxtaposition of open spaces and spaces defined by street furniture, landscaping, and low walls; landscaped areas not intended for occupancy; and individual seating. This design could be flexible enough to accommodate a large number of people when required for large events, or could be used for individual groupings of people.

A large, open space would encourage individuals and small groups to spread out rather than feel at ease nearer together. A heavily landscaped area would be attractive and would help define separate spaces for people to gather, but may limit the greatest number of people from assembling. An amphitheater would accommodate a large number of people but would be limited in flexibility for other types of informal uses.

**The answer is D.**

# TRANSPORTATION AND UTILITIES

20.   Assuming the building site shown is surrounded on four sides by city streets, which building and road layout is most appropriate for the site topography?

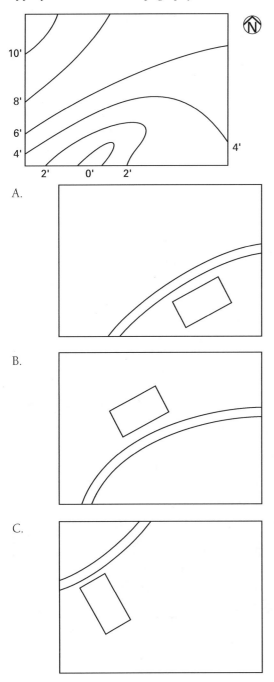

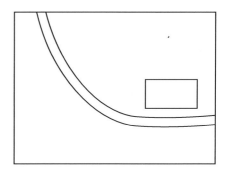

### Solution

Without knowing other conditions of the site, the best placement of the building and road is based on road grading and building construction on the existing topography. Roads should cut across slopes gradually to minimize steep grades, so this eliminates choice D where the road runs perpendicular to the slope. The road is well placed in C, but the length of the building runs perpendicular to the slope, which would make construction more difficult and expensive. Choice A works fairly well, with a gradual slope for the road and the building on level ground, but the road is in a valley and on the north side of the building. Choice B places the building parallel to the contour lines, is on a south-facing slope, and has a road gently rising across the grade with curves following the direction of the contours, so this is the best choice.

**The answer is B.**

21.   What is the minimum outside radius for an automobile cul-de-sac with no parking?

     A.   20 ft (6 m)
     B.   30 ft (9 m)
     C.   40 ft (12 m)
     D.   50 ft (15 m)

### Solution

40 ft (12 m) is the recommended minimum radius to accommodate current automobile sizes and turning radii.

**The answer is C.**

22.   The development of a middle-school campus is planned for a sparsely populated but growing suburban residential location. The city is planning new streets and property layouts around the school site, as shown. Two existing arterial streets border the site on the north and west as shown, and two new streets are proposed for the south (Evans Avenue) and east (10th Street) borders.

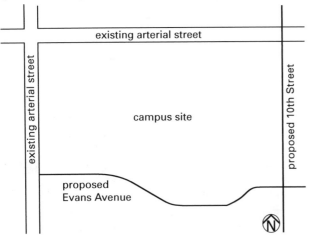

The school architect should recommend to the local planning board that the proposed streets be of which types?

    A.   Evans Avenue: local
           10th Street: local

    B.   Evans Avenue: local
           10th Street: collector

    C.   Evans Avenue: collector
           10th Street: collector

    D.   Evans Avenue: collector
           10th Street: arterial

### Solution

Local streets are intended to give direct access to building sites and are often curvilinear. At least one of these characteristics would be desirable for this property, and the street to the south (Evans Avenue) meets this requirement. In addition, Evans Avenue serves the longer dimension of the site, so there would be more opportunities to access the site from a local street on the south side of the property. Collector streets connect local streets and arterial streets, so 10th Street would best serve as a collector.

*Study Note:* Know the various types of streets and how they are used in urban planning, as well as some basic precepts of street layout such as vertical and horizontal alignment and intersection planning.

**The answer is B.**

23.   During the evaluation of a proposed construction site, the architect sketched the property lines, building location, existing sewer line in the adjacent street, and proposed location of the sanitary sewer connecting the building to the main line, as shown.

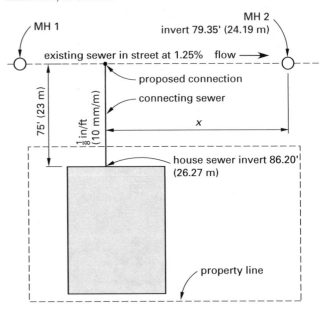

In order to determine if this site and building location are feasible for a sewer connection, what additional piece of information does the architect need?

    A.   the distance between MH 1 and MH 2

    B.   the distance $x$ between MH 2 and the connection point

    C.   the size of the connecting sewer line

    D.   the invert elevation of MH 1

### Solution

To calculate the invert elevation of the connection point to see if the connecting line would fall above or below the main line, determine the distance $x$ and then work backward from the invert elevation of manhole (MH) 2 using the slope of 1.25%. This will give the invert elevation of the main line where the connection will be made. The lowest point of the connecting sewer line can be calculated using the house sewer invert elevation, the 1/8 in/ft (10 mm/m) slope, and the 75 ft (23 m) distance.

The distance between MH 1 and MH 2 is irrelevant because the slope and one invert elevation are known. The size of the connecting sewer line does affect the minimum slope, but the slope is already given as 1/8 in/ft (10 mm/m). The invert elevation of MH 1 is also irrelevant because the slope and invert of MH 2 are known.

*Study Note:* This question requires an understanding of the importance of gravity flow in drainage and how to calculate slopes. Although this question does not require calculation of the invert elevation at the point of connection, it assumes a knowledge of what is required. The information needed is either the distance between two points and the elevation of the two points, or the elevation of one point, the slope, and the distance to the second point.

Be aware that a 1% slope is approximately $^1/_8$ in/ft (10 mm/m) and a 2% slope is approximately $^1/_4$ in/ft (20 mm/m).

### Terms to Know

*invert:* the low point or bottom of a pipe or manhole in a sewage system

**The answer is B.**

24. Which type of road needs the widest right-of-way?

    A. street
    B. main street
    C. avenue
    D. boulevard

### Solution

A boulevard consists of multilane roads in each direction with parking lanes, often separated by a planting median or with wide planting areas on both sides. Boulevards have right-of-ways of 100 ft (30 m) to 130 ft (40 m). A street is a small-scale, low-speed local connector road with a right-of-way of about 80 ft (24 m). An avenue is a short-distance, medium-speed road with a right-of-way about the same as a street. The term "main street" is generally not used to classify roadway types in transportation planning.

**The answer is D.**

25. Where are utilities commonly located?

    A. under streets
    B. anywhere in the right-of-way
    C. under sidewalks and curb lanes
    D. under streets or sidewalks

### Solution

Utilities are most commonly located anywhere in the right-of-way, away from buildable properties. In most cases, they are under the street portion of the right-of-way. When they must cross private property, they are usually located in utility easements, which are not buildable.

**The answer is B.**

## CIRCULATION AND PARKING

26. What area per car should be used to estimate the required size of a parking lot and related drives?

    A. 200 ft² (19 m²)
    B. 300 ft² (28 m²)
    C. 400 ft² (37 m²)
    D. 500 ft² (46 m²)

### Solution

300 ft² (28 m²) per car is typically used to estimate parking lot size if it includes the parking spaces, access, and fairly efficient driveways. 400 ft² (37 m²) per car can be used to estimate parking spaces, drives, and walkways.

**The answer is B.**

27. Local zoning regulations require 550 parking spaces for a large manufacturing plant and office facility. Parking, drives, and related walks must also be accounted for. For preliminary planning purposes, what is the minimum required parking lot size?

    A. 3 ac (1.2 ha)
    B. 4 ac (1.5 ha)
    C. 5 ac (2.0 ha)
    D. 6 ac (2.4 ha)

### Solution

For estimating purposes, use an area of 400 ft² (37 m²) per parking space. This value accounts for parking space, driveways, and walkways. For a parking lot of this size, you would need to allow for walks to provide safe access to the building.

Note that an area of 300 ft² (28 m²) per car is often used for just parking and driveways, but this question requires that walkways be included, and the size of the parking lot would also require additional drives, so a larger figure is needed.

Therefore,

*In U.S. units:*

$$\text{total parking area} = (\text{area per parking space})$$
$$\times (\text{number of spaces})$$
$$= \left(400 \frac{\text{ft}^2}{\text{space}}\right)(550 \text{ spaces})$$
$$= 220{,}000 \text{ ft}^2$$

Convert the area in square feet to acres.

$$\text{total parking area in acres} = \frac{220{,}000 \text{ ft}^2}{43{,}560 \frac{\text{ft}^2}{\text{ac}}}$$
$$= 5.05 \text{ ac} \quad (5 \text{ ac})$$

*In SI units:*

$$\text{total parking area} = \left(37 \frac{\text{m}^2}{\text{space}}\right)(550 \text{ spaces})$$
$$= 20\,350 \text{ m}^2$$

Convert the area in square meters to hectares.

$$\text{total parking area in hectares} = \frac{20\,350 \text{ m}^2}{10\,000 \frac{\text{m}^2}{\text{ha}}}$$
$$= 2.035 \text{ ha} \quad (2.0 \text{ ha})$$

*Study Note:* Know the rules of thumb for area per car and the number of square feet in an acre (hectare). For many large-scale projects, using an approximate value of 44,000 ft²/ac will solve the problem. (In SI units there are 10 000 m² in a hectare.)

**The answer is C.**

---

28.   The recommended minimum width for a sidewalk is _____ ft (_____mm). (Fill in the blank.)

### Solution

A 5 ft (1525) width allows two wheelchairs to pass traveling in opposite directions, provides for the minimum 5 ft turning diameter for wheelchairs, and generally allows other common types of use, such as two people walking side by side, people passing in opposite directions, and comfortable use of walkers and other mobility aids.

**The answer is 5 ft (1525 mm).**

29.   Which of the intersections shown would be best for laying out a two-way site access road?

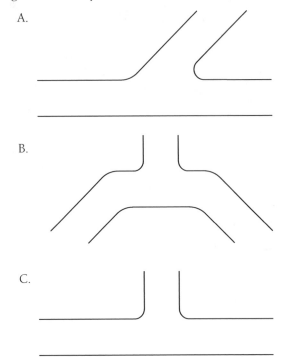

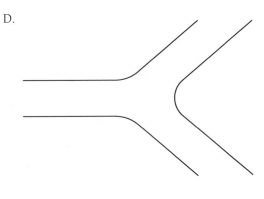

### Solution

Intersections should always be laid out as simply as possible. When two roads intersect, a 90° angle is best. When one road intersects another at an angle, the minimum angle is 80°.

The angle shown in choice A is too acute. The angled roads shown in choice B are too close to the intersecting road, which would make waiting and turning dangerous. Choice D is incorrect because two-way Y-intersections are inherently dangerous.

**The answer is C.**

30.   Which of the following would result in the best site circulation?

I.    planning the service entry drive separate from the automobile entry and drive
II.   making parking areas oversized to accommodate pedestrian circulation
III.  designing all two-way roads at least 24 ft wide
IV.   limiting parking area traffic to a single entrance away from pedestrian walks
V.    laying out walks parallel to parking areas

    A.   I, III, and IV
    B.   I, III, and V
    C.   II, IV, and V
    D.   I, III, IV, and V

*Solution*

Statement II is incorrect because automobile and pedestrian traffic should always be kept separate. Statement IV may be considered partially correct due to the idea of separating parking from walks, but a single entrance may create conflicts with vehicles pulling into and out of parking spaces and entering and leaving by the same drive. The other three statements are generally good guidelines for planning site circulation.

**The answer is B.**

31.   To determine the minimum parking requirements for site development, the architect should first consult

    A.   ADA-ABA Accessibility Guidelines
    B.   development covenants
    C.   the local building code
    D.   zoning regulations

*Solution*

Zoning regulations typically govern the minimum number of parking and loading spaces required on a site. This should be the first requirement that the architect researches. ADA-ABA Accessibility Guidelines gives requirements for the number, size, and configuration of accessible spaces, but this information can only be determined after the total number of parking spaces is established. Although not common, there may be additional requirements in covenants, but these would be determined after zoning regulations were determined. The building code in effect within a jurisdiction does not determine the required number of parking spaces.

**The answer is D.**

32.   If land is limited, which of the following is the best way to plan parking lots?

    A.   two-way circulation with 90° parking on both sides of a drive
    B.   30° parking on both sides of a one-way loop system
    C.   combining service circulation with parking at a 45° angle
    D.   90° parking on one side of a one-way circulation drive

*Solution*

90° parking layouts are always the most efficient if space is limited, so choices B and C are incorrect. Choice D is incorrect because a single-loaded circulation drive providing access to parking is not as efficient as two rows of parking sharing one drive.

**The answer is A.**

## CLIMATE AND SUSTAINABLE DESIGN

33.   The fraction of radiant energy reflected from a surface relative to the total radiant energy received by the surface is called

    A.   albedo
    B.   conductivity
    C.   insolation
    D.   radiant fraction

*Solution*

A surface's *albedo* is calculated as the reflected radiant energy divided by the total (received) radiant energy. Albedo can range from zero to 1.0. A surface with an albedo of 1.0 is a perfect mirror (all energy is reflected). A surface with an albedo of zero is a perfect black matte surface (all energy, or radiant heat, is absorbed).

*Conductivity* is the rate at which heat flows through a material. *Insolation* is the total solar radiation on a horizontal surface. Radiant fraction is not a real term.

**The answer is A.**

34.  In the Northern Hemisphere, the optimum tilt angle of an active solar collector for year-round use is approximately equal to the

  A.  solar altitude on the spring and fall equinoxes
  B.  solar altitude on the winter solstice
  C.  building's latitude
  D.  building's latitude plus 15°

*Solution*

The best orientation of solar panels, either for heating or photovoltaics, is approximately the latitude of the building location or slightly greater. For space heating systems, an angle of the latitude plus 15 degrees is optimum for the winter heating season.

**The answer is C.**

35.  For overall energy conservation and cost-effectiveness in a temperate climate, the most advantageous type of earth-sheltered building would be one that is

  A.  built into the side of a south-facing hill
  B.  above ground with earth bermed against all sides
  C.  above ground with a thick covering of earth and vegetation on the roof
  D.  completely underground with a central court that is open to the sky

*Solution*

A building built into a south-facing slope gains the advantages of an earth-sheltered structure (stable earth temperature, protection from cold north winds, and natural soundproofing), while keeping the south side open for passive solar energy use and minimizing the costs of earth moving.

Providing earth berms against four sides of an aboveground building increases costs for earth moving and decreases the opportunity to use the south facade for solar heat gain. A building with a vegetated roof cover, or "green roof," does reduce both heat gain and heat loss over the roof, but it costs more to build and does not help protect the sides of the building. Underground buildings with courtyards have the advantage of stable earth temperature but are expensive to build and have little window area.

**The answer is A.**

36.  A small building is being designed for a site in Minnesota. If it's desired to minimize reliance on mechanical systems, which of the following design strategies should be incorporated? (Choose the three that apply.)

  A.  maximize south-facing windows
  B.  incorporate high ceilings
  C.  design a compact form
  D.  use dark colors for the building exterior
  E.  minimize interior thermal mass
  F.  use evergreen trees on the south side of the building

*Solution*

Minnesota has a cool to cold climate. South-facing windows are good for passive solar heat gain. A compact form minimizes the surface area to reduce heat loss during the winter. Dark colors absorb more solar radiation than light colors.

Choice B is incorrect because, used with natural ventilation, high ceilings are more appropriate for a hot-humid climate. Choice E is incorrect because thermal mass should be maximized to take advantage of solar heat gain. In a cold climate it is desirable to have as much mass as possible to absorb and store the heat gathered during daylight hours for use at night.

Choice F is incorrect because deciduous trees, not evergreen, are desirable on the south side of the building to let in the sun during the winter.

**The answer is A, C, and D.**

37.  A row of trees of moderate density will reduce the wind velocity on the leeward side by about 30% to 40% up to about

  A.  three times the height of the trees
  B.  five times the height of the trees
  C.  seven times the height of the trees
  D.  nine times the height of the trees

*Solution*

For a row of trees of moderate density, wind speed is reduced about 30% to 40% on the leeward side up to a distance of about five times the tree height.

**The answer is B.**

38.   A small, three-story rectangular office building in a temperate climatic region is planned for the site shown. To simplify grading, the long dimension of the building will be placed parallel to the contour lines.

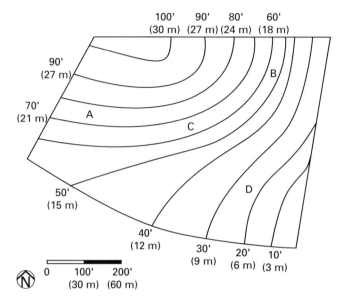

Which of the four locations indicated would be best suited for a building designed to demonstrate the application of passive solar heating?

    A.   location A
    B.   location B
    C.   location C
    D.   location D

*Solution*

For solar heating in a temperate climate, the best orientation for a rectangular building is with the long side positioned about 17° east of south. This orientation provides maximum radiant heat gain. Assuming that the building will be oriented parallel to the contours as stated in the question, the other locations on the site would tend to position the building in other directions.

> *Study Note:* Understand the basic planning guidelines for the four general climatic regions of the United States: cold or cool, temperate, hot-arid, and hot-humid. Most questions concerning climate refer to the temperate region, but an understanding of the design principles for any region is essential. Many of these principles are described in *Design with Climate,* by Victor Olgyay.

**The answer is C.**

39.   Potential overheating of a medical clinic in a temperate climate could be minimized by

    A.   designing an overhang for the west and east sides of the building
    B.   planning a building shape to minimize the surface area of south-facing walls
    C.   having a landscape architect specify deciduous trees near the south elevation
    D.   all of the above

*Solution*

Choice A is incorrect because overhangs are not effective on the west and east sides of a building due to the low sun angle. Vertical louvers, or fins, are more effective in these locations. Choice B is incorrect because the south side actually receives less solar radiation than the east or west sides because the sun is high during the middle of the day. It would be more effective to minimize the roof area to cut down on solar radiation.

**The answer is C.**

## LEGAL AND ECONOMIC INFLUENCES

40.   What term describes a land measure that is 6 mi on a side?

    A.   section
    B.   check
    C.   township
    D.   range

*Solution*

A *township*, as used by the U.S. Public Land Survey System, is a square unit of land 6 mi on a side. It is subdivided into 36 *sections*, each one a square mile. A *check* is a square 24 mi on a side consisting of 16 townships.

**The answer is C.**

41.   Under the IBC, what is the maximum allowable floor area of a sprinklered, two-story, Type III B, Group B occupancy building that has access on 20% of its perimeter?

    A.   38,000 ft$^2$
    B.   57,000 ft$^2$
    C.   76,000 ft$^2$
    D.   114,000 ft$^2$

*Solution*

From IBC Table 503 (Table 55.7 in *ARE Review Manual*), the basic allowable floor area for a one-story building of B occupancy, type III-B construction is 19,000 ft². If the building is fully sprinklered, the allowable area per floor can be doubled for multi-storied buildings, so the maximum allowable floor area is 38,000 ft². The basic area can be multiplied by the number of stories up to three, so the maximum total allowable area is 76,000 ft².

**The answer is C.**

42.    The owner of the lot shown wants to develop a building with the maximum allowable gross area.

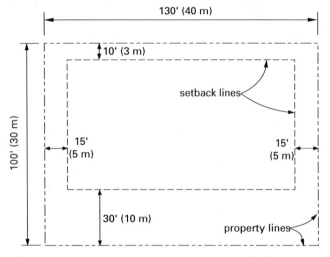

The floor area ratio (FAR) is 2.0. The owner wants to build each story fully to the setback lines shown. The building can have a maximum of _____ stories. (Fill in the blank.)

*Solution*

*In U.S. units:*

If the floor area ratio (FAR) is 2.0, then the maximum amount of floor area that can be built is two times the area of the entire lot. The area of the lot is

$$\text{lot area} = (100 \text{ ft})(130 \text{ ft}) = 13{,}000 \text{ ft}^2$$

Then the maximum floor area for the entire building is

$$\text{total floor area} = (\text{lot area})(\text{FAR})$$
$$= (13{,}000 \text{ ft}^2)(2.0)$$
$$= 26{,}000 \text{ ft}^2$$

Next, determine the available buildable area within the setbacks. The distance between the side setbacks is

$$130 \text{ ft} - 15 \text{ ft} - 15 \text{ ft} = 100 \text{ ft}$$

The distance between the front and rear setbacks is

$$100 \text{ ft} - 30 \text{ ft} - 10 \text{ ft} = 60 \text{ ft}$$

The available area for each floor, then, is

$$\text{floor area per story} = (100 \text{ ft})(60 \text{ ft})$$
$$= 6000 \text{ ft}^2$$

To find the allowable number of stories, divide the maximum floor area for each story into the maximum total area.

$$\text{number of stories} = \frac{\text{total floor area}}{\text{floor area per story}}$$
$$= \frac{26{,}000 \text{ ft}^2}{6000 \ \dfrac{\text{ft}^2}{\text{story}}}$$
$$= 4.33 \text{ stories}$$

Each story will contain the full 6000 ft² allowed, so the building can have a maximum of four stories.

*In SI units:*

If the floor area ratio (FAR) is 2.0, then the maximum amount of floor area that can be built is two times the area of the entire lot. The area of the lot is

$$\text{lot area} = (30 \text{ m})(40 \text{ m}) = 1200 \text{ m}^2$$

Then the maximum floor area for the entire building is

$$\text{total floor area} = (\text{lot area})(\text{FAR})$$
$$= (1200 \text{ m}^2)(2.0)$$
$$= 2400 \text{ m}^2$$

Next, determine the available buildable area within the setbacks. The distance between the side setbacks is

$$40 \text{ m} - 5 \text{ m} - 5 \text{ m} = 30 \text{ m}$$

The distance between the front and rear setbacks is

$$30 \text{ m} - 10 \text{ m} - 3 \text{ m} = 17 \text{ m}$$

The available area for each floor, then, is

$$\text{floor area per story} = (30 \text{ m})(17 \text{ m})$$
$$= 510 \text{ m}^2$$

To find the allowable number of stories, divide the maximum floor area for each story into the maximum total area.

$$\text{number of stories} = \frac{\text{total floor area}}{\text{floor area per story}}$$
$$= \frac{2400 \text{ m}^2}{510 \ \dfrac{\text{m}^2}{\text{story}}}$$
$$= 4.71 \text{ stories}$$

Each story will contain the full 510 m² allowed, so the building can have a maximum of four stories.

**The answer is 4 stories.**

43.    According to ADA-ABA Accessibility Guidelines, what is the maximum allowable vertical change of level on an accessible route without using a ramp or bevel?

   A.   $^1/_8$ in (3.2)
   B.   $^1/_4$ in (6.5)
   C.   $^3/_8$ in (9.5)
   D.   $^1/_2$ in (13)

*Solution*

Changes in level up to $^1/_4$ in (6.5) may be made without using a ramp or bevel. Changes in level from $^1/_4$ in (6.5) to $^1/_2$ in (13) may be made with a vertical portion $^1/_4$ in (6.5) high and with the remaining distance beveled at a 1:2 slope. Any change in level $^1/_2$ in (13) or greater must be made with a ramp or curb ramp that has a maximum slope of 1:12, or else employ an elevator or platform lift.

**The answer is B.**

44.    Which of the following would have the LEAST effect on the maximum height of a building?

   A.   bulk plane restrictions
   B.   floor area ratios
   C.   zoning setbacks
   D.   occupancy group

*Solution*

Although zoning setbacks may indirectly influence building height, they have the least effect of the four answer choices. Floor area ratios limit the total gross buildable area based on lot size, but when the maximum buildable area is placed within the restriction of zoning setbacks, the building height is thus determined. Bulk plane restrictions limit the area beyond which a building can pass, which often limits the total height.

In the building codes, a building's occupancy group of and construction type determine the maximum building area, the maximum height in feet (meters), and the maximum number of stories.

**The answer is C.**

45.    An accessible route must serve

   A.   all accessible spaces and parts of a building
   B.   the corridors, stairs, elevators, and toilet rooms of a building
   C.   entrances, parking, toilet rooms, corridors, and drinking fountains
   D.   those areas where physically disabled people are likely to need access

*Solution*

By definition, any part of a building that is required to be accessible must be accessible from the entrance of the building.

**The answer is A.**

46.    Which of the following are typically regulated by zoning ordinances? (Choose the four that apply.)

   A.   how a property is used
   B.   types of exterior materials
   C.   floor area ratios
   D.   number of loading spaces
   E.   minimum amount of window exposure
   F.   distances from property line to building

*Solution*

Exterior material types are not regulated by zoning ordinances, though they may be governed by covenants, development restrictions, and to some extent by building codes. Zoning ordinances do not regulate either minimum or maximum window area.

**The answer is A, C, D, and F.**

47.    Which of the following areas of a building are considered parts of the means of egress?

I.     storeroom
II.    corridor
III.   enclosed stairway
IV.    exterior courtyard
V.     public sidewalk

   A.   I, II, and III
   B.   II, III, and IV
   C.   I, II, III, and IV
   D.   I, II, III, IV, and V

### Solution

Option V is not part of the means of egress because it is an example of the public way. All of the other building areas listed are part of the exit access, the exit, or the exit discharge.

**The answer is C.**

48.   The owner of the lot shown wants to develop a building with the maximum allowable gross area.

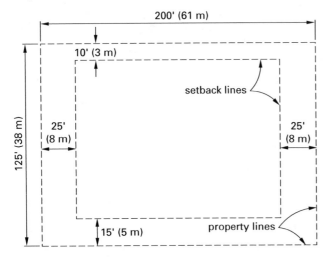

If the floor area ratio (FAR) is 3.0 and the owner builds each story to the setback lines shown, the building will be _____ stories.

### Solution

If the floor area ratio (FAR) is 3.0, the maximum amount of floor area that can be built is three times the area of the lot. To find the allowable number of stories, divide the available ground area, $A$, within the setbacks into the maximum allowable floor area.

*In U.S. units:*

First, find the maximum building floor area allowed by the floor area ratio.

$$\text{maximum building floor area} = (\text{area of the lot})(\text{FAR})$$
$$= (25{,}000 \text{ ft}^2)(3.0)$$
$$= 75{,}000 \text{ ft}^2$$

Next, determine the available ground area within the setbacks that can be used for building.

$$A = (\text{width between side setbacks})$$
$$\times (\text{width between front and rear setbacks})$$
$$= (150 \text{ ft})(100 \text{ ft})$$
$$= 15{,}000 \text{ ft}^2$$

Finally, find the allowable number of stories by dividing the maximum building floor area by the available ground area.

$$\text{number of stories} = \frac{\text{maximum building floor area}}{A}$$
$$= \frac{75{,}000 \text{ ft}^2}{15{,}000 \dfrac{\text{ft}^2}{\text{story}}}$$
$$= 5 \text{ stories}$$

*In SI units:*

First, find the maximum building floor area allowed by the floor area ratio.

$$\text{maximum building floor area} = (2318 \text{ m}^2)(3.0)$$
$$= 6954 \text{ m}^2$$

Next, determine the available buildable area within the setbacks that can be used for building.

$$A = (45 \text{ m})(30 \text{ m})$$
$$= 1350 \text{ m}^2$$

Finally, find the allowable number of stories by dividing the maximum building floor area by the available ground area.

$$\text{number of stories} = \frac{6954 \text{ m}^2}{1350 \dfrac{\text{m}^2}{\text{story}}}$$
$$= 5.15 \text{ stories} \quad (5 \text{ stories})$$

**The answer is 5 stories.**

49. Setback distances are determined by a city's

    A. building code
    B. zoning code
    C. development agency
    D. planning office

*Solution*

Setbacks are established by the zoning code of a city or county.

    *Study Note:* Know the various aspects of land use that zoning does control: allowable uses, the amount of land that can be covered with buildings, bulk of structures, setback distances, and parking and loading space requirements.

**The answer is B.**

50. The maximum allowable area of a building is limited by a combination of

    A. floor area ratio and construction type
    B. occupancy group and setback requirements
    C. bulk plane limits and floor area ratio
    D. construction type and setback requirements

*Solution*

Zoning regulations limit total building area based on floor area ratio and setbacks, while building codes limit building area by construction type and occupancy group. Bulk plane limits may affect the area by limiting height in some cases, but they are not a primary determinant. Of the choices given, the floor area ratio (from zoning codes) and construction type (from building codes) would be the combination that limits maximum area.

**The answer is A.**

51. What factors determine the total allowable area and height of a building? (Choose the four that apply.)

    A. construction type
    B. occupancy group
    C. number of exits from the building
    D. separation between adjacent buildings
    E. combustibility of exterior materials
    F. whether or not the building has a sprinkler system

*Solution*

The basic allowable floor area and height of a building are determined by the construction type and the occupancy group. This basic allowable floor area may be increased according to certain criteria, such as if the building is fully sprinklered and/or if there is a certain amount of space around the building.

**The answer is A, B, D, and F.**

52. A property's boundaries are commonly described with

    A. metes and bounds
    B. reference to a section and township
    C. location within a subdivision
    D. all of the above

*Solution*

All three of these methods are commonly used to describe property, although the metes and bounds method is not used as much as the other two methods.

**The answer is D.**

# OTHER SITE DESIGN INFLUENCES

53. Of the following remedial actions, which would most effectively provide a cooler microclimate for an existing building over the long term?

    A. Plant deciduous trees to the south of the building.
    B. Move the asphalt parking lot on the south to the east, and replace it with vegetation.
    C. Build a pond on the windward side of the building.
    D. Plant coniferous trees on the west side of the building.

*Solution*

Moving the parking lot and replacing it with vegetation would reduce the albedo (amount of solar radiation reflected). This would in turn reduce the amount of heat reflected onto the building, for the most effective solution.

**The answer is B.**

54.    An architect can best discourage criminal activity in a street-level apartment lobby by applying which of the following design strategies?

    A.   separating the lobby and the street with a large expanse of glass

    B.   changing the paving texture at the property line

    C.   clearly marking the entrance with a "Residents Only" sign

    D.   adding a bright light over the entrance door

*Solution*

Although all these design features would help discourage criminal activity, the best approach would be to make activity inside the lobby visible from the street. This employs the principal of natural surveillance.

Changing the texture of the flooring between the sidewalk and the private property, using a sign, and adding a light are methods of territorial reinforcement, but they would not be as effective as opening the lobby to public view.

> *Study Note:* Review the theories of defensible space, which include the basic concepts of surveillance, territoriality, and symbolic barriers. These were originally described by Oscar Newman in *Defensible Space* and later expanded in *Creating Defensible Space*. A link to a free downloadable copy of *Creating Defensible Space* in PDF format can be found at **www.ppi2pass.com/resources.html**. Some of the concepts are also summarized in the section on "Crime Prevention through Environmental Design" in *Architectural Graphic Standards*, by Charles George Ramsey, et al. Refer to the Recommended Reading list for additional resources. The ideas of defensible space have spawned the newer term "crime prevention through environmental design" (CPTED).

**The answer is A.**

55.    Which of the following is NOT an effective security strategy for the exterior of a retail store?

    A.   provide two entrances on opposite sides of the facade

    B.   minimize the number of signs on the front windows

    C.   place the cash-wrap area near the front of the store

    D.   keep the exterior of the store well lit

*Solution*

It more difficult to secure a site with two entrances on opposite sides of a retail facade than it is to secure a single entry point. A single, strong entry is not only easier to supervise, but also improves security through territorial reinforcement. The other strategies would be effective security measures.

**The answer is A.**

56.    An architect is developing a site plan for a building that is adjacent to a highway. Which of the following strategies is best for attenuating noise?

    A.   maximize the distance between the new building and the highway

    B.   construct a masonry wall as high as possible next to the highway

    C.   plant a combination of deciduous and evergreen trees 100 ft (30 m) deep

    D.   locate the building as far from the highway as possible and plant a row of evergreen trees

*Solution*

All of the strategies listed would help mitigate the noise problem, but building a solid, high, mass wall would be the most effective.

Although increasing the distance between a noise source and the receiver helps to reduce the sound level, it would not make a significant difference in this case. While noise from a point source decreases as the square of the distance increases, noise from a linear source, such as a highway, only decreases directly as the distance increases. Doubling the distance would only decrease the sound level by about three decibels, which is barely noticeable.

Trees help attenuate sound, but only if they are planted in a deep row and if a combination of deciduous and evergreen trees is used. A deep row of trees consists of several rows perpendicular to the direction of the sound. The greater the number of rows, the better the sound attenuation will be. Planting a combination of deciduous and evergreen trees is helpful because their different densities attenuate different sound frequencies. However, trees are most effective in attenuating sound at higher frequencies and may not be very useful in dealing with the low frequencies of highway noise.

**The answer is B.**

57. In regard to blast security, the space between a building and the outermost secured perimeter is called the

    A. blast reduction zone
    B. perimeter defense area
    C. security setback
    D. standoff distance

*Solution*

The standoff distance is the space between a building and the potential location of a blast threat. For blast protection, this distance should be maximized, because blast energy decreases exponentially with increased distance between the source of the blast and the building.

**The answer is D.**

58. An architect is developing a site plan for a developed property with an existing building. The building is in good condition and was used for the same purpose as the client's proposed use of the site. Which of the following four strategies would earn the greatest number of points within the LEED 2009 for New Construction rating system?

    A. maintain at least 50% of the interior nonstructural elements
    B. remove the building and recycle and/or salvage at least 50% of construction and demolition debris
    C. maintain at least 95% of the existing walls, floors, and roof
    D. reuse materials from the site that amount to 5%, by cost, of the total value of materials on the project

*Solution*

If 95% or more of the existing building's structure, exterior walls, and roof are reused, the LEED 2009 NC rating system awards three points, one point each for reaching levels of 55%, 75%, and 95% (MR Credits 1.1 through 1.3). Window assemblies and nonstructural roofing material are excluded from these calculations.

(Under the older LEED NC rating system v2.2, two points were awarded, for 75% and 95%.)

In the LEED 2009 NC rating system, each of the other three strategies—maintaining 50% of the interior nonstructural elements (MR Credit 1.4), recycling and/or salvaging 50% of debris (MR Credit 2.1), and reusing materials from the site worth 5%, by cost, of the total value of materials (MR Credit 3.1)—would earn only one point.

**The answer is C.**

59. Which of the following is NOT a method of estimating the volume of cut and fill?

    A. contour area method
    B. end area method
    C. elevation estimation
    D. calculation by grid

*Solution*

Elevation estimation is not a method of estimating cut and fill.

The contour area method is based on a contour drawing showing the areas to be cut and filled. Because the volume of earth that must be moved is proportional to the sums of the areas, this method can give a quick visual representation of amounts. For more detailed analysis, the volume of each area can be calculated based on the contour interval and by using manual or computer-aided means to mathematically calculate volumes and compare cut and fill.

The end area method is similar to the contour method except the individual volumes to be calculated are assumed to have parallel vertical faces rather than horizontal faces as with the contour method. This method is often used for doing cut-and-fill calculations for roadways.

The calculation by grid method involves drawing a square grid over the site and determining the existing and new elevations at each grid intersection. The volume change of each grid can be calculated with positive amounts representing fill and negative amounts representing cut.

**The answer is C.**

60. In the diagrammatic section shown, it is important to keep angles A and B within certain limits so as to

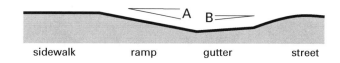

    A. allow for accessibility
    B. keep stormwater runoff within acceptable limits
    C. provide an easy transition for pedestrians
    D. allow bicycles to use the sidewalk

*Solution*

The relationship between these two angles is important because if the transition between one slope and an opposing counterslope is too great, wheelchair users will have difficulty moving across them. In extreme cases, the footrests or anti-tip wheels on the wheelchair may not clear the surface, or the user could flip over backwards. ADA-ABA Accessibility Guidelines limit the slope of curb ramps to 1:12 and the slope of counterslopes to 1:20.

**The answer is A.**

61.    The contour lines in the sketch shown would typically indicate

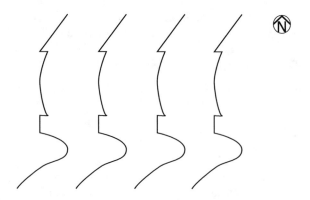

   A.   a sidewalk sloping down from east to west with a berm on the south side

   B.   a road with drainage in the middle and a sidewalk and berm on the south

   C.   a swale adjacent to a walking path sloping from northeast to southwest

   D.   a curbed street sloping up from west to east next to a drainage ditch

*Solution*

This pattern is characteristic of roads with a crown in the middle sloping toward curbs on either side. As with any contour map, contour lines representing a ridge (which is what a crown of a road is in miniature) point in the direction of the downslope, so this road slopes down from east to west (or up from west to east as the answer choice states). The contours pointing in the other direction represent a ditch. Just as with any valley on a contour map, the lines point in the direction of the upslope.

**The answer is D.**

# SITE DESIGN VIGNETTE

## Directions

Develop a schematic site plan based on a program that includes legal requirements and other site influences.

The base plan presents a site on which to place buildings, related site elements, and vegetation in relation to orientation and environmental conditions. On this plan, draw and locate the following elements.

- two buildings
- an outdoor space
- required parking spaces (universally accessible spaces must be clearly indicated)
- vehicular access and service drives
- pedestrian walkways
- vegetation

Before beginning, review the program and the plan of the vacant site.

## Program

A developer plans to build a video store, restaurant, deck, and parking area on the site shown.

1. Locate a one-story, 20 ft (6.1 m) high restaurant close to the wetlands area. Use a block 50 ft by 80 ft (15.2 m by 24.4 m).

2. Locate a one-story, 15 ft (4.6 m) high video store close to the intersection of Stuart Street and 5th Avenue. Use a block 50 ft by 90 ft (15.2 m by 27.4 m).

3. Draw a 1500 ft² (140 m²) outdoor dining deck for the restaurant.

4. The restaurant deck must have a view of the wetlands area.

5. The view of the service entrance of the restaurant shall be blocked from both streets and from the site to the south.

6. The entrance of the restaurant shall receive noonday summer sun.

7. The restaurant deck shall be blocked from the prevailing winds by trees or buildings as appropriate.

8. Draw a total of 24 parking spaces.

   - 21 standard 9 ft by 18 ft (2.7 m by 5.5 m) parking spaces are required.

   - 3 universally accessible 12 ft by 18 ft (3.7 m by 5.5 m) parking spaces are required.

- Locate the parking area near the video store within the building limit lines. Locate the universally accessible parking spaces within 80 ft (24.4 m) of the main entrance of the video store. Accessible parking for the restaurant is provided in the existing parking area to the south of the site.

- All parking spaces shall be perpendicular to the traffic aisles.

- No parallel parking is permitted.

9. Connect the parking area, including the accessible parking spaces, the video store entrance, and the sidewalk along 5th Avenue with a continuous pedestrian walkway system. Connect the parking area, the restaurant entrance, the sidewalk along 5th Avenue, and the parking area to the south of the property with a continuous pedestrian walkway system. The restaurant deck may be considered part of the walkway system. The accessible parking spaces DO NOT have to be connected with the restaurant. The video store and restaurant do not have to have direct pedestrian connection, but both should connect to the parking area.

10. Draw vehicular circulation on the site from 5th Avenue to access the parking area and the service entrance to the restaurant. The service drive shall attach to the service entrance of the restaurant.

    - All drives and traffic aisles shall be 24 ft (7.3 m) wide.

    - Drive-through circulation in the parking area is required.

    - Dead-end parking is prohibited.

    - The service drive must not pass through the parking area.

    - No turnaround or drive-through circulation is required for service vehicles.

    - Only one curb cut on 5th Avenue is allowed, no closer than 140 ft (42.7 m) from the south curb line of Stuart Street. The intersection of the access drive with the street must be perpendicular to the street for at least the first 20 ft (6.1 m) of the drive.

11. The following general conditions also apply.

    - No built improvement can occur within the setbacks, except that driveways and sidewalks can cross setbacks to connect to public walks and streets.

    - Provide a 30 ft (9.1 m) setback from the property line adjacent to the wetlands area.

- Assume a 50 ft (15.2 m) height for all trees.
- No more than five existing trees may be removed or disturbed.

## Tips

- Be sure to check the number of trees that have been disturbed or removed. On the actual exam, use the check tool to do this.
- On the actual exam, roads and walkways are polylines. The *move group* tool can be used to move them, and the *move, adjust* tool can be used to adjust them.
- On the actual exam, it may be easier to erase a road and begin again than to keep trying to adjust it.
- Use the *move group* tool to move a bank of parking spaces.
- For parking spaces laid out on an angle, it is more precise to lay them out orthogonally, then rotate. However, it is best to keep parking spaces oriented either horizontally or vertically.
- If one of two overlapping elements cannot be selected, keep clicking without moving the mouse until the desired element is highlighted.

## Warnings

- On the actual exam, the dashed centerline of a driveway must connect to the dashed centerline of a road or another driveway for the two elements to count as connected.
- A walkway must be attached to another element in order to count as connected to it.
- On the actual exam, parking spaces will not be counted as universally accessible unless the handicap spaces tool is used.

## Tools

Useful tools include the following.
- *zoom* tool for adjusting driveways or walkways
- *sketch line* tool and *sketch circle* tool to align and measure spaces and to determine clearances

**Target Time:** 1.5 hours

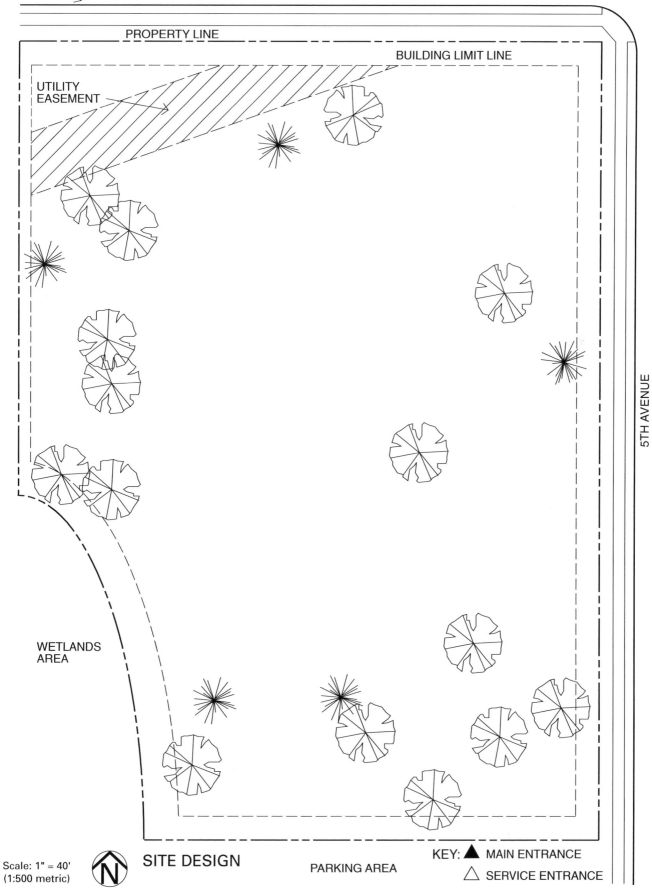

WINDS

STUART STREET

PROPERTY LINE

BUILDING LIMIT LINE

UTILITY
EASEMENT

5TH AVENUE

WETLANDS
AREA

Scale: 1" = 40'
(1:500 metric)

SITE DESIGN

PARKING AREA

KEY: ▲ MAIN ENTRANCE

△ SERVICE ENTRANCE

## SITE DESIGN:
## PASSING SOLUTION

This is a very good solution. The buildings have been placed according to the program while respecting the set-back lines and the wetlands setback requirement. The parking area has been laid out correctly with the correct number of spaces and with the accessible spaces within the required distance from the video store. All required pedestrian circulation has been properly provided including the connection with the parking area to the south. The restaurant entrance is facing south and the deck has the required view of the wetlands. The deck and the service entrance are shielded by evergreen trees as suggested by the program. No more than five existing trees have been disturbed. Although the sidewalk leading to 5th Avenue is partially drawn under two trees the program will not count this as a disturbance if just a portion of the walk is under the drip line. To be safe, do not place more than half of a walkway within the drip line.

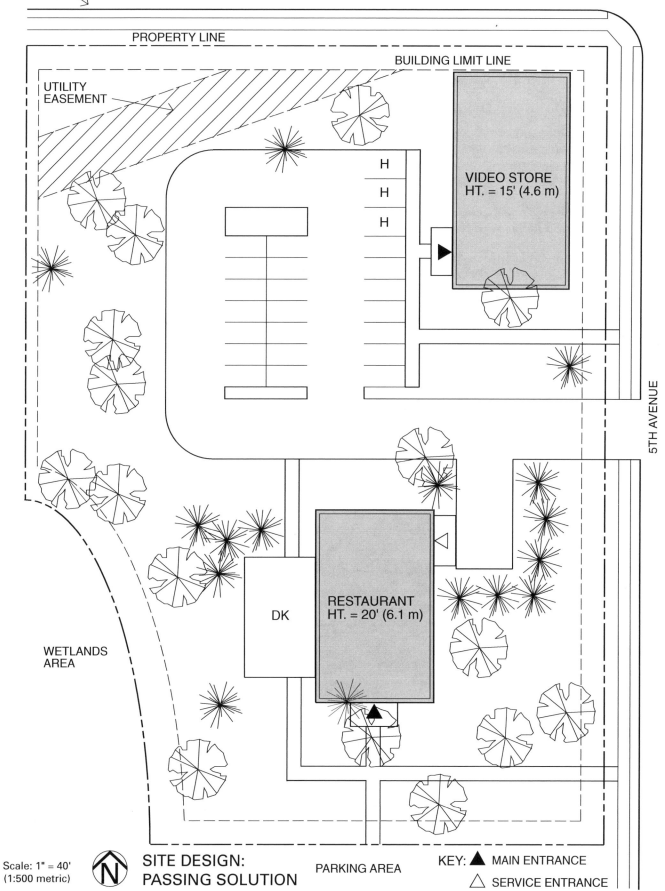

WINDS

STUART STREET

PROPERTY LINE

BUILDING LIMIT LINE

UTILITY
EASEMENT

VIDEO STORE
HT. = 15' (4.6 m)

H
H
H

▶

5TH AVENUE

RESTAURANT
HT. = 20' (6.1 m)

DK

WETLANDS
AREA

◁

▲

Scale: 1" = 40'
(1:500 metric)

N

SITE DESIGN:
PASSING SOLUTION

PARKING AREA

KEY: ▲ MAIN ENTRANCE
△ SERVICE ENTRANCE

## SITE DESIGN:
## FAILING SOLUTION

In this solution the buildings are placed appropriately except that the restaurant deck is located within the wetlands setback area. The parking area is laid out to satisfy the program requirements, although the separate circulation drive is inefficient because it does not serve any parking spaces. However, this is not enough to fail the solution. The driveway curb cut is too close to the south curb line of Stuart Street. The deck area for the restaurant is less than required by the program and there is no pedestrian access from the restaurant to 5th Avenue. Also note that although the restaurant entrance receives noonday summer sun, it faces slightly to the east. While this is not enough to fail the solution, it is generally best to face any required element that requires noonday sun directly to the south.

New trees have been placed properly but seven existing trees have been disturbed, two more than allowed by the program. The drip lines of the two trees at the end of the parking area have also been encroached on. Note that when any program in the ARE calls for trees not to be disturbed, this means that a tree should not be disturbed anywhere within its drip line, not just at its trunk. However, the program will allow some tolerance for slight overlaps so these two trees would not be considered a conflict. If a slight overlap occurs the check tool should be used to verify that the program does not consider it a disturbance.

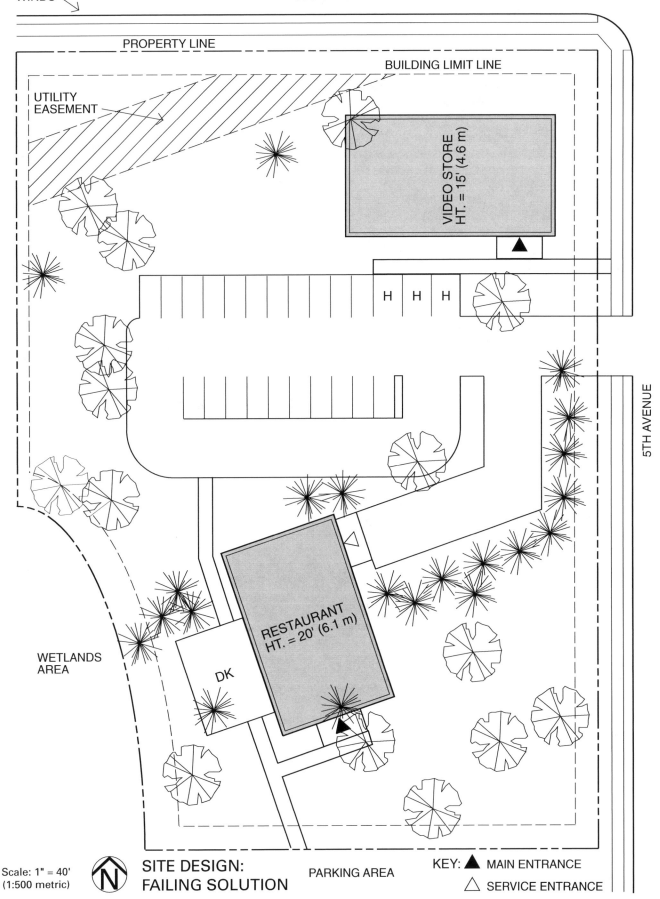

WINDS

STUART STREET

PROPERTY LINE

BUILDING LIMIT LINE

UTILITY
EASEMENT

VIDEO STORE
HT. = 15' (4.6 m)

H   H   H

5TH AVENUE

WETLANDS
AREA

DK

RESTAURANT
HT. = 20' (6.1 m)

Scale: 1" = 40'
(1:500 metric)

N

SITE DESIGN:
FAILING SOLUTION

PARKING AREA

KEY: ▲ MAIN ENTRANCE
     △ SERVICE ENTRANCE

## SITE GRADING VIGNETTE

### Directions

The site plan that follows is a topographic representation of an existing site. A built object is to be placed on the site and the site is to be regraded. The completed plan should show both the built object and the reworked contour lines that will cause water to flow from the site in accordance with the program and site conditions.

Before beginning, review the program and the existing contour lines and site conditions.

### Program

A flat picnic pad is to be located within a defined area of a public park. Building is restricted within a limit line within the parcel boundary as shown on the site plan.

1.  Place a 30 ft by 50 ft (9 m by 15 m) paved picnic pad within the building limit line. Regrade the site to create a level area for the picnic pad. Indicate the finish elevation of the pad. The finish elevation must be 6 in (0.15 m) above the level area.

2.  Regrade the site so that water will flow around and away from the picnic pad. The slope of the regraded areas shall be at least 1% and no more than 20%. Manipulating the contour lines outside the building limit line and inside the parcel boundary is permitted.

3.  Existing trees and the location of the proposed bicycle path shall not be disturbed. Contour lines within tree drip lines shall not be disturbed.

4.  Changes in contour lines that are not required for proper drainage should be avoided.

### Tips

- Use the sketch tools to draw the object, the drainage lines wanted, and the minimum separation of contour lines.
- The *erase* tool affects all changes that have been made to a contour line. Undo affects the last action only.

**Target Time:** 30 minutes

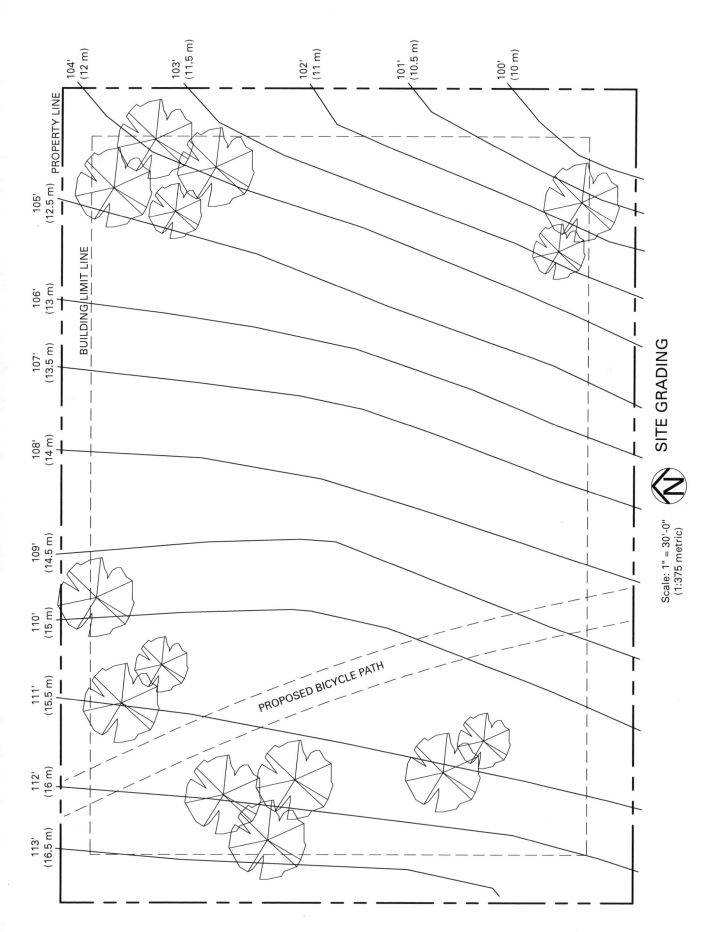

PROPERTY LINE

104' (12 m)
103' (11.5 m)
102' (11 m)
101' (10.5 m)
100' (10 m)

105' (12.5 m)

BUILDING LIMIT LINE

106' (13 m)

107' (13.5 m)

108' (14 m)

109' (14.5 m)

110' (15 m)

111' (15.5 m)

PROPOSED BICYCLE PATH

112' (16 m)

113' (16.5 m)

SITE GRADING

Scale: 1" = 30'-0"
(1:375 metric)

## SITE GRADING: PASSING SOLUTION

This vignette requires the examinee to place an object of a given size within a site and readjust existing contour lines to control water flow while conforming to specific site requirements.

### Solving Approach

Step 1   Begin by estimating the most likely place for the picnic pad. Generally, the object required by the program should be placed in approximately the middle of the open space available for building, to give sufficient room for manipulating contour lines. The contours below the object usually have to be manipulated more than those above the object, so it may help to place the object off center toward the higher portion of the site. In many cases it works best to orient the longer dimension of the object roughly parallel with the contour lines.

Step 2   Begin with the high point of that portion of the site that needs to be regraded. Starting here, a swale must be created to divert water away from the picnic area. Remember that the contour lines of swales, or valleys, "point" uphill. The contour line that is manipulated to start the swale (that is, the highest contour line to be changed) will loop around the object on its downhill side to create the level area on which the object sits.

Step 3   Progressing downhill, continue forming swales with the contour lines so that water from higher areas is kept from flowing onto the pad. If this proves difficult, the initial contour line that forms the level area for the built object may need to be moved uphill or downhill.

Step 4   When changing contour lines, do not disturb contours where they cross existing objects or pass within the drip lines of trees. In this example, contours through the proposed bicycle path cannot be disturbed.

Step 5   Verify that no two contours are close enough together to form a slope greater than 20% or far enough apart to form a slope less than 1%. In this case, with 1 ft (0.5 m) contours, no two contours can be closer together than 5 ft (2.5 m) or farther apart than 100 ft (50 m).

Step 6   Mark the elevation of the picnic pad 6 in (0.15 m) above the flat graded area.

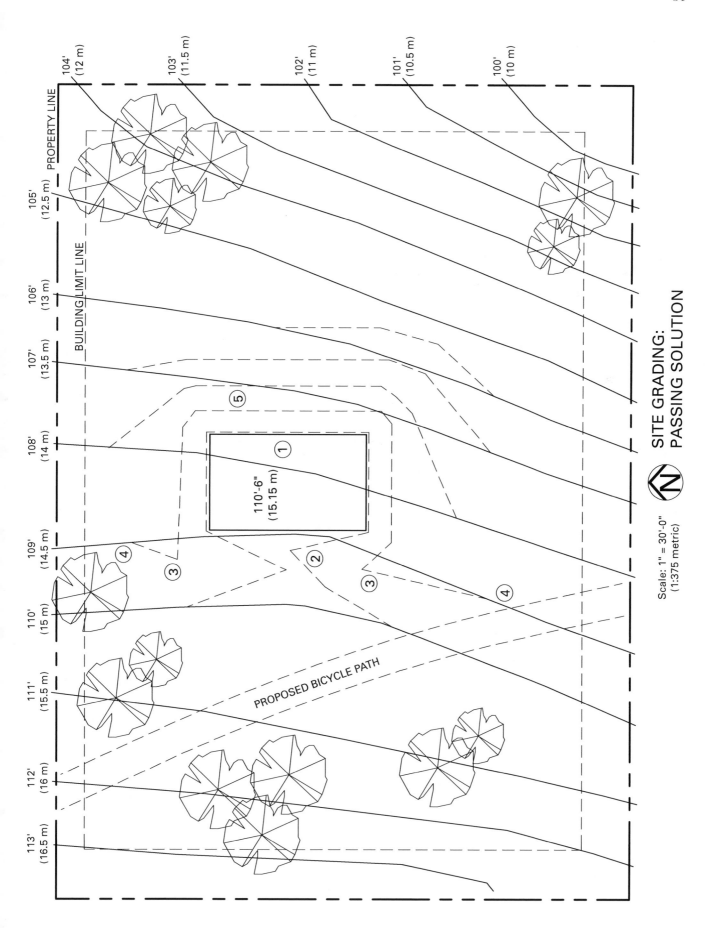

SITE GRADING:
PASSING SOLUTION

Scale: 1" = 30'-0"
(1:375 metric)

# SITE GRADING:
# FAILING SOLUTION

## Pitfalls

Note 1   The graded area for the pad is not level. It slopes from contour 105 (12.5 m) up to contour 106 (13 m).

Note 2   Contours 104 and 105 (12 m and 12.5 m) are too close, resulting in a slope exceeding 20%.

Note 3   The grade line is disturbed under the drip line of the tree.

Note 4   Although an attempt has been made to create a swale on the high side of the pad, water is diverted onto the pad. There is a 106 ft (13 m) grade directly next to the 105 ft 6 in (12.65 m) elevation of the pad.

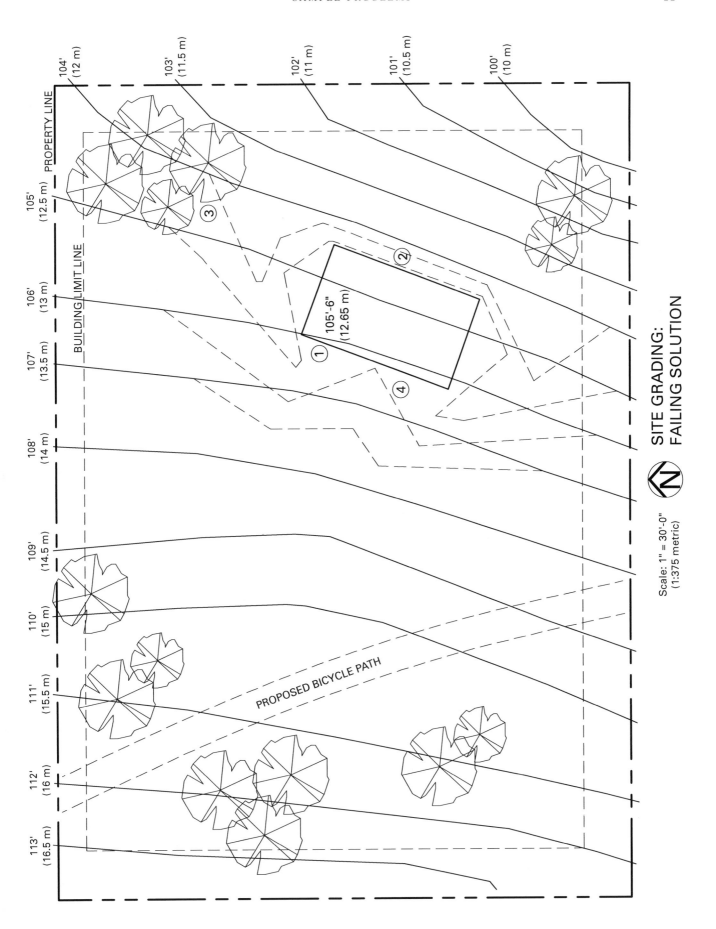

104' (12 m)
103' (11.5 m)
102' (11 m)
101' (10.5 m)
100' (10 m)

PROPERTY LINE

105' (12.5 m)

BUILDING LIMIT LINE

③

②

106' (13 m)

105'-6"
(12.65 m)

①

107' (13.5 m)

④

108' (14 m)

SITE GRADING:
FAILING SOLUTION

Scale: 1" = 30'-0"
(1:375 metric)

109' (14.5 m)

110' (15 m)

111' (15.5 m)

PROPOSED BICYCLE PATH

112' (16 m)

113' (16.5 m)

# PRACTICE EXAM: MULTIPLE CHOICE

## Directions

Reference books should not be used on this practice exam. Besides this book, you should have only a calculator, pencils, and scratch paper. (On the actual exam, these will be provided and should not be brought into the site.)

**Target Time:** 1.5 hours

| | | | |
|---|---|---|---|
| 1. Ⓐ Ⓑ Ⓒ Ⓓ | 26. Ⓐ Ⓑ Ⓒ Ⓓ | 51. Ⓐ Ⓑ Ⓒ Ⓓ | |
| 2. Ⓐ Ⓑ Ⓒ Ⓓ | 27. Ⓐ Ⓑ Ⓒ Ⓓ | 52. Ⓐ Ⓑ Ⓒ Ⓓ Ⓔ Ⓕ | |
| 3. Ⓐ Ⓑ Ⓒ Ⓓ | 28. Ⓐ Ⓑ Ⓒ Ⓓ | 53. Ⓐ Ⓑ Ⓒ Ⓓ | |
| 4. Ⓐ Ⓑ Ⓒ Ⓓ | 29. Ⓐ Ⓑ Ⓒ Ⓓ | 54. _____ | |
| 5. Ⓐ Ⓑ Ⓒ Ⓓ Ⓔ Ⓕ | 30. Ⓐ Ⓑ Ⓒ Ⓓ | 55. Ⓐ Ⓑ Ⓒ Ⓓ | |
| 6. Ⓐ Ⓑ Ⓒ Ⓓ | 31. Ⓐ Ⓑ Ⓒ Ⓓ | 56. Ⓐ Ⓑ Ⓒ Ⓓ | |
| 7. Ⓐ Ⓑ Ⓒ Ⓓ | 32. Ⓐ Ⓑ Ⓒ Ⓓ | 57. Ⓐ Ⓑ Ⓒ Ⓓ | |
| 8. Ⓐ Ⓑ Ⓒ Ⓓ | 33. Ⓐ Ⓑ Ⓒ Ⓓ | 58. _____ | |
| 9. Ⓐ Ⓑ Ⓒ Ⓓ | 34. Ⓐ Ⓑ Ⓒ Ⓓ Ⓔ Ⓕ | 59. Ⓐ Ⓑ Ⓒ Ⓓ Ⓔ Ⓕ | |
| 10. Ⓐ Ⓑ Ⓒ Ⓓ | 35. Ⓐ Ⓑ Ⓒ Ⓓ | 60. Ⓐ Ⓑ Ⓒ Ⓓ | |
| 11. Ⓐ Ⓑ Ⓒ Ⓓ | 36. Ⓐ Ⓑ Ⓒ Ⓓ | 61. Ⓐ Ⓑ Ⓒ Ⓓ | |
| 12. Ⓐ Ⓑ Ⓒ Ⓓ | 37. Ⓐ Ⓑ Ⓒ Ⓓ | 62. Ⓐ Ⓑ Ⓒ Ⓓ | |
| 13. Ⓐ Ⓑ Ⓒ Ⓓ | 38. Ⓐ Ⓑ Ⓒ Ⓓ | 63. Ⓐ Ⓑ Ⓒ Ⓓ | |
| 14. Ⓐ Ⓑ Ⓒ Ⓓ | 39. Ⓐ Ⓑ Ⓒ Ⓓ | 64. Ⓐ Ⓑ Ⓒ Ⓓ | |
| 15. Ⓐ Ⓑ Ⓒ Ⓓ | 40. Ⓐ Ⓑ Ⓒ Ⓓ | 65. Ⓐ Ⓑ Ⓒ Ⓓ | |
| 16. Ⓐ Ⓑ Ⓒ Ⓓ | 41. Ⓐ Ⓑ Ⓒ Ⓓ | | |
| 17. Ⓐ Ⓑ Ⓒ Ⓓ | 42. Ⓐ Ⓑ Ⓒ Ⓓ | | |
| 18. Ⓐ Ⓑ Ⓒ Ⓓ | 43. Ⓐ Ⓑ Ⓒ Ⓓ | | |
| 19. Ⓐ Ⓑ Ⓒ Ⓓ | 44. Ⓐ Ⓑ Ⓒ Ⓓ | | |
| 20. Ⓐ Ⓑ Ⓒ Ⓓ | 45. Ⓐ Ⓑ Ⓒ Ⓓ | | |
| 21. Ⓐ Ⓑ Ⓒ Ⓓ Ⓔ Ⓕ | 46. Ⓐ Ⓑ Ⓒ Ⓓ Ⓔ Ⓕ | | |
| 22. Ⓐ Ⓑ Ⓒ Ⓓ | 47. Ⓐ Ⓑ Ⓒ Ⓓ | | |
| 23. Ⓐ Ⓑ Ⓒ Ⓓ | 48. Ⓐ Ⓑ Ⓒ Ⓓ | | |
| 24. Ⓐ Ⓑ Ⓒ Ⓓ | 49. Ⓐ Ⓑ Ⓒ Ⓓ | | |
| 25. Ⓐ Ⓑ Ⓒ Ⓓ | 50. Ⓐ Ⓑ Ⓒ Ⓓ | | |

1.    In most climatic regions, the most energy-efficient orientation for a rectangular building is with the long axis

   A.   approximately 45° east of south
   B.   approximately 15° east of south
   C.   due south
   D.   approximately 20° west of south

2.    When determining the required area for a leaching field, the architect should require a

   A.   percolation test
   B.   potability test
   C.   topographic survey
   D.   water table determination

3.    Which of the following would NOT be a consequence of inadequate water runoff control during and after construction?

   A.   accelerated soil creep
   B.   erosion of stream banks
   C.   decreased runoff coefficient
   D.   increased load on the storm sewer system

4.    A continuous perforated pipe placed near the footing of a foundation is called a

   A.   French drain
   B.   leader line
   C.   strip drain
   D.   trench drain

5.    Which of the following sustainable strategies best manages stormwater runoff? (Choose the three that apply.)

   A.   bioswales
   B.   catch basins
   C.   cisterns
   D.   infiltration basins
   E.   pervious paving
   F.   box culverts

6.    What type of soil would be best for slab-on-grade construction?

   A.   clayey sand
   B.   organic silt
   C.   poorly graded gravel
   D.   lean clay

7.    What is the minimum width for a two-lane road designed for two-way traffic?

   A.   18 ft (5.5 m)
   B.   20 ft (6.1 m)
   C.   24 ft (7.3 m)
   D.   28 ft (8.5 m)

8.    The architect can minimize the heat island effect of impervious site paving by selecting a material with

   A.   low albedo
   B.   high albedo
   C.   low conductivity
   D.   high conductivity

9.    Which schematic site section shown here demonstrates the best approach for reducing noise from an adjacent site?

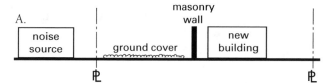

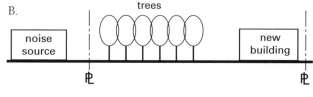

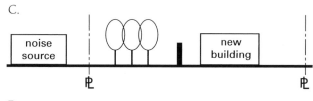

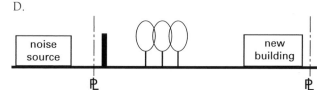

10. An architect is planning an infill building in an urban setting. To maintain the continuity of the public space enclosure defined by the other buildings, the architect should be most sensitive to the

    A. building height

    B. recess line

    C. setback

    D. transition line

11. Which of the following statements regarding blast-resistant design is FALSE?

    A. Laminated glass is an effective protective strategy.

    B. Blast energy decreases in inverse proportion to the cube of the distance.

    C. L-shaped buildings can minimize blast effects.

    D. Standoff distance should be maximized.

12. An architect is laying out the house sewer for a small commercial building. The sewer has been sized at 6 in (152) in diameter with a 1/8 in/ft (10 mm/m) slope. The architect discovers that the original information on the invert of the main sewer line, which is approximately 300 ft (91 m) away, was incorrect and that it is actually 1 ft (305) higher than planned. What would be the LEAST expensive course of action?

    A. decrease the slope and increase the size of the house sewer

    B. angle the house sewer to connect farther down the main line

    C. change the location of the building

    D. decrease the slope of the sewer and add an intermediate manhole

13. In the diagram shown, which section represents a valley?

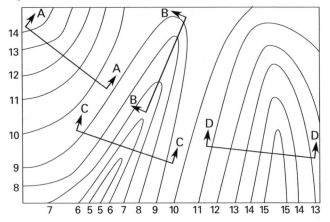

    A. section A-A

    B. section B-B

    C. section C-C

    D. section D-D

14. The maximum area of signage on the exterior of a building is most commonly regulated by

    A. building codes

    B. restrictive covenants

    C. state laws

    D. zoning ordinances

15. What is the minimum recommended width for a two-way driveway off a local or collector street?

    A. 18 ft (5.5 m)

    B. 20 ft (6.1 m)

    C. 24 ft (7.3 m)

    D. 30 ft (9.1 m)

16. What standard test is used to determine the optimum compaction of site fill?

    A. Proctor test

    B. pit test

    C. dry sample boring test

    D. soil load test

17.   A building site with the dimensions shown has set-backs of 25 ft (10 m) on all four sides. If the allowable FAR is 3.0, which building footprint would be best for sustainable design?

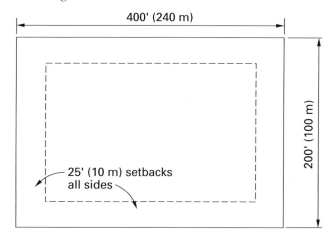

400' (240 m)

200' (100 m)

25' (10 m) setbacks
all sides

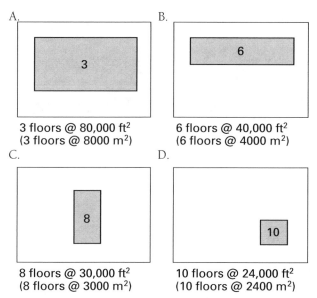

A.

3

3 floors @ 80,000 ft²
(3 floors @ 8000 m²)

B.

6

6 floors @ 40,000 ft²
(6 floors @ 4000 m²)

C.

8

8 floors @ 30,000 ft²
(8 floors @ 3000 m²)

D.

10

10 floors @ 24,000 ft²
(10 floors @ 2400 m²)

18.   In planning the location of a building on a site, the location of which of the following utilities should be considered first?

    A.   water main

    B.   sanitary sewer

    C.   underground telephone line

    D.   power line

19.   Which of the following frontage types would cause accessibility problems if used in urban street design?

    A.   arcade

    B.   forecourt

    C.   porch and fence

    D.   stoop

20.   The most efficient parking space configuration is one in which vehicles are parked at an angle relative to the driving lane of

    A.   30°

    B.   45°

    C.   60°

    D.   90°

21.   To determine the regulations that pertain to a planned development around a wetlands area, which of the following should the architect investigate? (Choose the three that apply.)

    A.   local governmental rules

    B.   local building codes

    C.   state governmental rules

    D.   U.S. Army Corps of Engineers regulations

    E.   development covenants

    F.   zoning ordinances

22.   Which building type would be most appropriate for a retail store in an urban setting?

    A.   courtyard building

    B.   perimeter yard building

    C.   rear yard building

    D.   side yard building

23.   Which schematic layout would be most appropriate for a site in a neighborhood dominated by Baroque planning concepts?

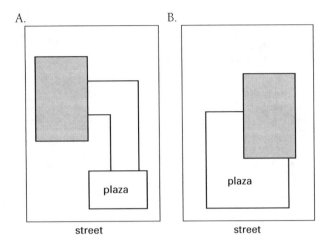

24.   According to ADA-ABA Accessibility Guidelines, what is the maximum slope for a curb cut?

A.   1:6
B.   1:8
C.   1:10
D.   1:12

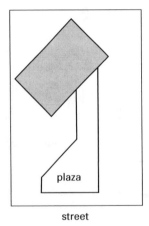

25.   Which of the following is a poor strategy for minimizing light pollution on a site?

A.   eliminate parking lot lighting
B.   employ light bollards instead of pole-mounted luminaires
C.   specify low-reflectance surfaces
D.   use full cutoff luminaires

26.   In the illustration shown, what would be the best use for the sloped region between points A and B?

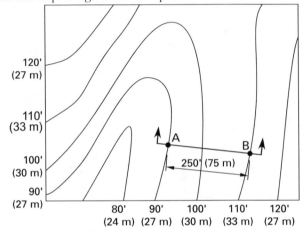

A.   use it for parking
B.   use it for walks and buildings
C.   landscape it to stabilize the soil
D.   develop terraces with retaining walls

27.   On the fall equinox in the Northern Hemisphere, the sun

A.   is at its northernmost position
B.   is at its southernmost position
C.   rises at its earliest time and sets at its latest
D.   rises and sets over the equator

28.   A public road that connects expressways is

A.   a service road
B.   a local street
C.   a collector street
D.   an arterial street

29.   An architect is planning a development project near a major river. If the owner requires that there be no risk of flooding in the development, the architect needs to determine the

    A.   local flood plain regulations
    B.   NFIP standards
    C.   probable maximum flood (PMF)
    D.   standard projected flood (SPF)

30.   The maximum permissible cross slope for a sidewalk as defined by ADA-ABA Accessibility Guidelines is

    A.   0.5%
    B.   1%
    C.   2%
    D.   4%

31.   The slope of a masonry or stone retaining wall is called the

    A.   batter
    B.   crib angle
    C.   rake
    D.   repose

32.   The basic allowable floor area of a planned building, as established by the building code in force, may be increased by adding a sprinkler system and

    A.   increasing the hourly fire protection of exterior walls
    B.   increasing the amount of open space between the building and the property lines
    C.   decreasing the square footage of openings in the exterior walls
    D.   reducing the height of the building

33.   According to the principles of crime prevention through environmental design (CPTED), which of the following is the LEAST useful strategy?

    A.   adding security guards at critical points
    B.   placing bars on ground floor windows
    C.   using territorial reinforcement
    D.   employing electronic methods of protection

34.   Which of the following should be included on a site survey requested by the architect? (Choose the four that apply.)

    A.   suggested view planes
    B.   location and width of easements
    C.   land contours
    D.   utilities requiring removal
    E.   position of existing roads adjacent to the site
    F.   location of existing buildings on the site

35.   According to ADA-ABA Accessibility Guidelines, what is the maximum permitted slope for accessible parking areas?

    A.   1%
    B.   2%
    C.   5%
    D.   8.33%

36.   The minimum distance from a property line to a building is primarily determined by

    A.   building codes
    B.   bulk plane covenants
    C.   fire zone requirements
    D.   zoning regulations

37.   During the site design phase of an urban project, where would the architect most likely find information regarding the location of electrical and telephone lines?

    A.   from the civil engineer
    B.   from the electrical engineer
    C.   from the utility companies
    D.   on technical maps maintained by the municipal government

38.   LEED points for new construction can be earned for all the following site development strategies EXCEPT

    A.   reducing construction activity pollution
    B.   redeveloping a brownfield
    C.   reducing light pollution
    D.   locating close to public transportation

39.    Which of the following sewer types would NOT carry blackwater?

    A.  building
    B.  house
    C.  sanitary
    D.  storm

40.    An architect is designing an exterior pedestrian walk. In one area, there is a change in level of 12 in (305). The transition must be made within a horizontal distance of no more than 14 ft (4267). Which of the following design solutions would be most appropriate?

    A.  two steps with 6 in (152) risers
    B.  three steps with 4 in (102) risers
    C.  a ramp 14 ft (4267) long
    D.  two steps with 6 in (152) risers and a ramp 12 ft (3658) long

41.    An architect plans a large building on an urban site. The length of the building is placed along the property line at the sidewalk and aligned with the street's other buildings. This is an example of creating

    A.  a path
    B.  a district
    C.  a node
    D.  an edge

42.    View plane restrictions are typically governed by

    A.  building codes
    B.  easements
    C.  local ordinances
    D.  zoning restrictions

43.    What type of electronic security system would best protect the exterior of an office building?

    A.  audio alarms
    B.  motion sensors
    C.  thermal detectors
    D.  video surveillance

44.    What is the minimum recommended width of a planting strip used to plant trees?

    A.  4–5 ft (1220–1525 mm)
    B.  6–7 ft (1830–2130 mm)
    C.  8–10 ft (2440–3050 mm)
    D.  10–12 ft (3050–3660 mm)

45.    Which of the following is NOT a requirement for making a site accessible for egress purposes?

    A.  An egress court or dispersal area must be provided.
    B.  Abrupt changes in level cannot exceed $1/4$ in (6).
    C.  Sidewalks must have a slope no greater than 1:20.
    D.  The cross slope of accessible routes must be no greater than 1:50.

46.    Which site design elements for fire protection are the responsibility of the architect? (Choose the four that apply.)

    A.  position and size of building canopies
    B.  surface material outside of the building
    C.  traffic control fences and bollard positions
    D.  maximum fire hydrant spacing on the street
    E.  utility poles and overhead utility lines
    F.  width of fire apparatus access drives

47.    Which of the following CANNOT be built over a utility easement?

    A.  access drive
    B.  landscaping strip
    C.  sidewalk
    D.  storage shed

48.    According to the Secretary of the Interior's Standards for Rehabilitation, which of the following modifications can usually be made to a historic property undergoing rehabilitation treatment?

    A.  repairing an existing but damaged exterior cornice molding
    B.  removing nonbearing interior walls to make larger spaces
    C.  chemical cleaning of brick and masonry
    D.  removing additions to the building that were made after original construction

49. In a residential subdivision, which of the following would be LEAST effective in reducing the potential for criminal activity?

A. using low plantings to define property lines
B. positioning exterior entry doors visible to the street or neighbors
C. designing stairways within solid structures
D. locating common areas within the view of a number of residential windows

50. How many square feet (m²) are in one acre (hectare)?

A. 41,520 ft² (100 m²)
B. 42,720 ft² (1,000 m²)
C. 43,560 ft² (10,000 m²)
D. 45,260 ft² (100,000 m²)

51. An architect is considering using a ground source heat pump to supply the heating for a moderate-size house. Which of the following is the most important factor in determining the feasibility of this type of heating system?

A. solar orientation of the house
B. size of the lot
C. average ground temperature
D. microclimate of the site

52. Which of the following are effective strategies for sustainability during preliminary site planning? (Choose the four that apply.)

A. select a suitable greenfield site
B. minimize the building footprint
C. position buildings along land contours
D. provide maximum lawn area
E. locate buildings and parking close to roads
F. reserve areas for infiltration basins

53. Which of the following is NOT a good design strategy for a building in a hot-arid climate?

A. using a compact form
B. shading all openings
C. minimizing thermal mass
D. minimizing opening sizes

54. The slope between points A and B is ____% (Fill in the blank.)

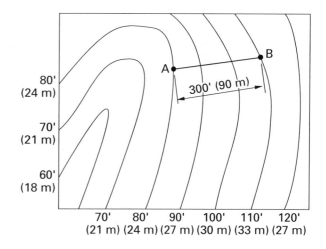

55. The most important characteristic of an on-site road designed to serve parking areas and service vehicles is the

A. slope
B. tangent
C. horizontal alignment
D. vertical alignment

56. The first zoning ordinance in the United States was passed in

A. 1791 in Washington, DC
B. 1793 in Philadelphia
C. 1876 in Boston
D. 1916 in New York City

57. During the design of a small retail building, an architect discovers that the building design exceeds the maximum height allowed by 18 in (457) and that reducing the building's height is impossible. The architect should suggest that the owner apply for

A. a conditional use permit
B. an easement
C. a PUD
D. a variance

58.  In the lot shown, if the FAR is 2.0, the maximum allowable gross buildable area is _____ ft² (_____m²). (Fill in the blank.)

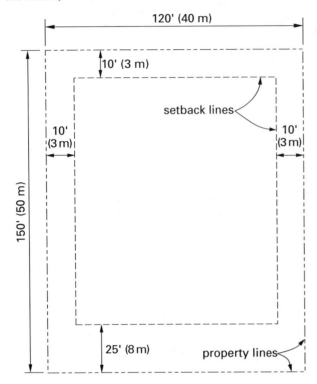

59.  An architect receives a soil report indicating the possibility of hydrostatic water problems surrounding a basement foundation. What construction techniques or materials should the architect consider using? (Choose the four that apply.)

    A.  dampproofing membrane

    B.  geotextiles

    C.  gravel fill below the floor slab

    D.  pervious paving around the building

    E.  positive slope away from the building

    F.  sump pumps

60.  The figure shown represents a plot of land.

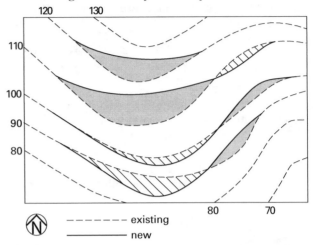

This diagram

    A.  is an earthwork diagram

    B.  shows areas unsuitable for building

    C.  shows desired positions for solar access

    D.  shows regrading options

61.  An architect is studying several sites for possible development by a client. Of the following sites, the one most likely to be buildable is

    A.  a designated wetland

    B.  a brownfield

    C.  in a floodplain

    D.  an endangered species habitat

62.  Which of the following outdoor deck materials would be most comfortable and best moderate the microclimate around a house in a temperate zone?

    A.  red brick pavers

    B.  light colored concrete

    C.  grass between stone pavers

    D.  dark wood decking

63. Four schematic parking lot layouts are shown. Assuming all parking spaces, drives, and access aisles are sized correctly, which layout would best serve a strip mall?

A.
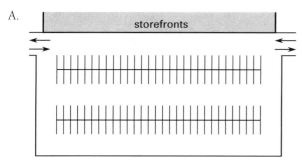

B.
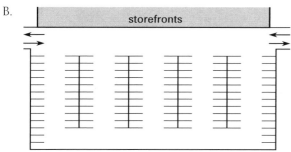

C.
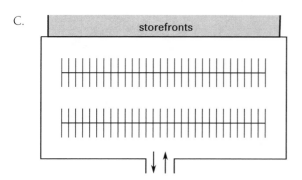

D.
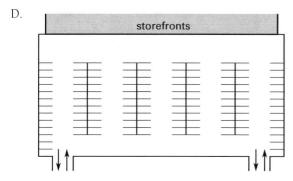

64. According to ADA-ABA Accessibility Guidelines, what is the minimum width of an accessible van parking space?

A. 96 in (2440)
B. 102 in (2590)
C. 120 in (3050)
D. 132 in (3350)

65. Which of the following is used to prevent sediment runoff during construction?

A. bioswale
B. riprap
C. screen grating
D. silt fence

# PRACTICE EXAM: VIGNETTES

—◇◇◇◇—

**Target Time:** two vignettes in 2 hours

## SITE DESIGN

### Directions

Develop a schematic site plan based on a program that includes legal requirements and other site influences.

The base plan that follows presents a site on which to place buildings, related site elements, and vegetation in relation to orientation and environmental conditions. On this plan, draw and locate the following elements.

- two buildings
- an outdoor space
- required parking spaces (universally accessible spaces must be clearly indicated)
- vehicular access and service drives
- pedestrian walkways
- vegetation

Before beginning, review the program and the plan of the vacant site.

### Program

A developer plans to build an apartment building, café/bookstore, pedestrian plaza, and parking area on the site shown.

1.  Locate a one-story, 20 ft (6.1 m) high café/bookstore near the lake. Use a block 50 ft by 70 ft (15.2 m by 21.3 m) as shown on the diagram.

    - The main entrance of the café/bookstore shall open directly onto the pedestrian plaza.

2.  Locate a five-story, 55 ft (16.8 m) high apartment building close to the café/bookstore. Use a block 70 ft by 100 ft (21.3 m by 30.5 m) as shown on the diagram.

    - The main entrance of the apartment building shall open directly onto the pedestrian plaza.

3.  Draw a 7000 ft² (650 m²) outdoor pedestrian plaza.

    - Locate the pedestrian plaza within the building limit lines so that the main entrances to both the café/bookstore and the apartment open directly onto the pedestrian plaza.

4.  The pedestrian plaza and café/bookstore must each have a view of the lake.

5.  The view of the service entrance of the café/bookstore shall be blocked from both streets and from the pedestrian plaza.

6.  The entrance of the café/bookstore shall receive noonday summer sun.

7.  The pedestrian plaza shall be blocked from the prevailing winds by trees or buildings as appropriate.

8.  Draw a total of 33 parking spaces as follows.

    - 30 standard 9 ft by 18 ft (2.7 m by 5.5 m) parking spaces are required.

    - Three universally accessible 12 ft by 18 ft (3.7 m by 5.5 m) parking spaces are required.

    - The universally accessible parking spaces must be within 100 ft (30.5 m) of the main entrance of the apartment.

    - All parking spaces shall be perpendicular to the traffic aisles.

    - No parallel parking is permitted.

9.  Connect the pedestrian plaza, the universally accessible parking spaces, and the main entrances of the two buildings to each other and to the existing public walk with a continuous walkway system.

    - The pedestrian plaza shall be considered part of the walkway system.

47

10. Draw vehicular circulation to connect the parking area and the service entrance to the street. The service drive shall attach to the service entrance of the café/bookstore.

- All drives and traffic aisles shall be 24 ft (7.3 m) wide.
- Drive-through circulation in the parking area is required.
- Dead-end parking is prohibited.
- The service drive must not pass through the parking area.
- No turnaround or drive-through circulation is required for the service drive.
- Only one curb cut is allowed, and it may be no closer than 120 ft (36.6 m) to the intersection of the centerlines of the two existing public streets.
- The intersection of the access drive with the street must be perpendicular to the street for at least the first 20 ft (6.1 m) of the drive.

11. The following general conditions also apply.

- No built improvement can occur within the setbacks, except that driveways and sidewalks can cross setbacks to connect to public walks and streets.
- Paving on the site shall be minimized.
- A setback of 80 ft (24.4 m) from the lake to any building improvements must be provided.
- Buildings must be separated by a minimum of 20 ft (6.1 m).
- Drives, traffic aisles, and parking spaces shall be no closer than 5 ft (1.5 m) to a building.
- Assume a 50 ft (15.2 m) height for all trees.
- No more than six existing trees may be removed or disturbed.

## Diagrams

The trees that shall be used as vegetation are shown in the diagrams following.

## Tips

- Be sure to check the number of trees that have been disturbed or removed. On the actual exam, use the *check* tool to do this.
- On the actual exam, roads and walkways are polylines. The *move group* tool can be used to move them, and the *move, adjust* tool can be used to adjust them.
- On the actual exam, it may be easier to erase a road and begin again than to keep trying to adjust it.

- Use the *move group* tool to move a bank of parking spaces.
- For parking spaces laid out on an angle, it is more precise to lay them out orthogonally, then rotate. However, it is best to keep parking spaces oriented either horizontally or vertically.
- If one of two overlapping elements cannot be selected, keep clicking without moving the mouse until the desired element is highlighted.

## Warnings

- On the actual exam, the dashed centerline of a driveway must connect to the dashed centerline of a road or another driveway for the two elements to count as connected.
- A walkway must be attached to another element in order to count as connected to it.
- On the actual exam, parking spaces will not be counted as universally accessible unless the handicap spaces tool is used.

## Tools

Useful tools include the following.

- *zoom* tool for adjusting driveways or walkways
- *sketch line* tool and *sketch circle* tool to align and measure spaces and to determine clearances

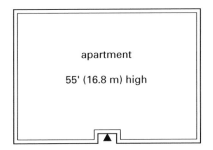

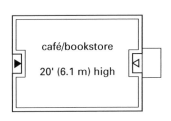

building plans

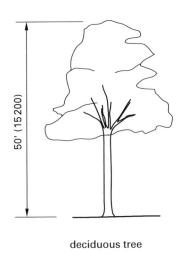

deciduous tree

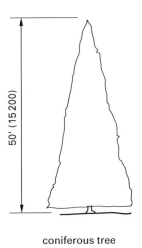

coniferous tree

tree elevations

site design elements

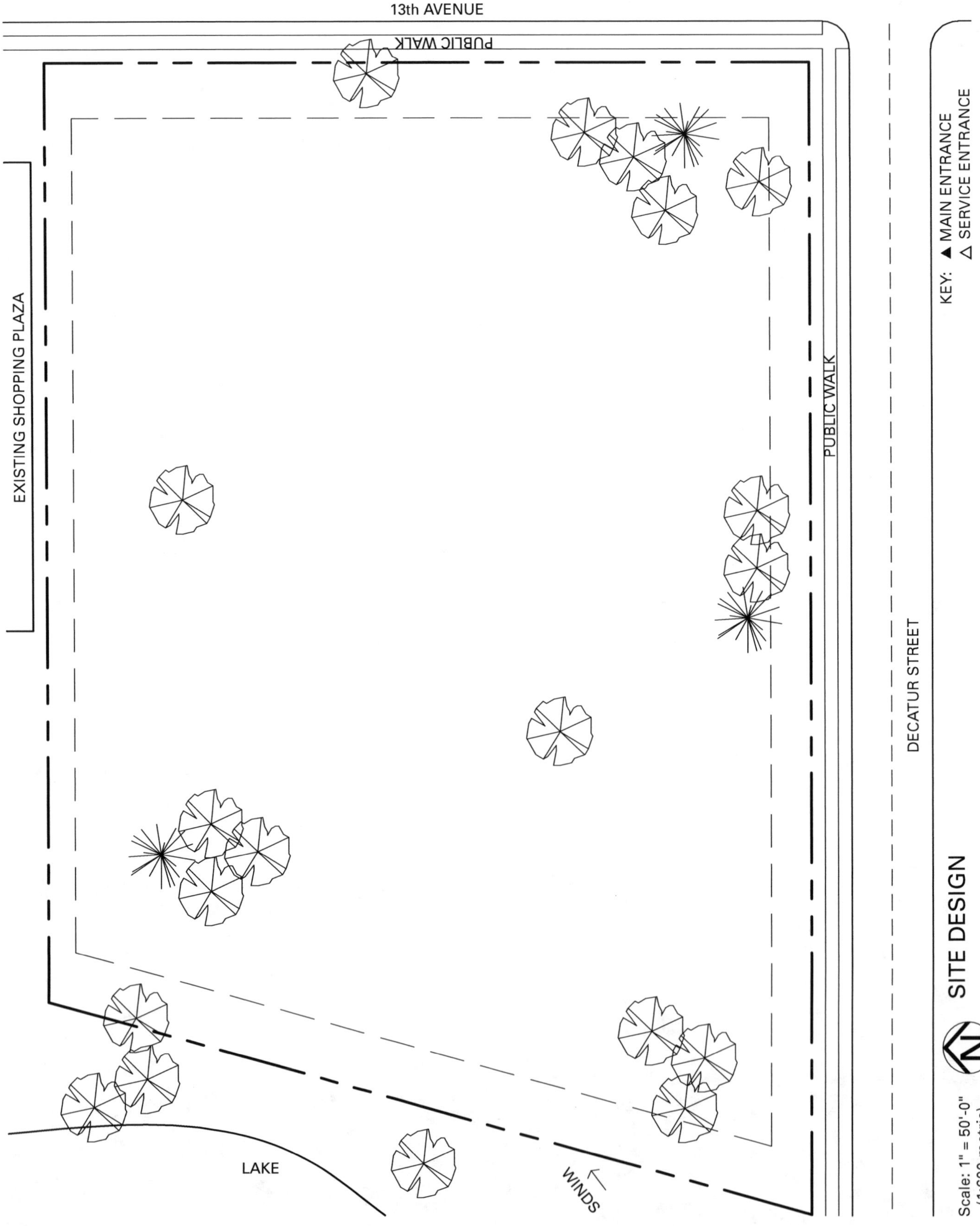

13th AVENUE

PUBLIC WALK

EXISTING SHOPPING PLAZA

PUBLIC WALK

DECATUR STREET

LAKE

WINDS

KEY:  ▲ MAIN ENTRANCE
      △ SERVICE ENTRANCE

SITE DESIGN

Scale: 1" = 50'-0"
(1:600 metric)

# SITE GRADING

## Directions

The site plan that follows is a topographic representation of an existing site. A built object is to be placed on the site and the site is to be regraded. The completed plan should show both the built object and the reworked contour lines that will cause water to flow from the site in accordance with the program and site conditions.

Before beginning, review the program and the existing contour lines and site conditions.

## Program

A flat viewing platform is to be located in a small park to highlight a scenic view to the south. The park is surrounded by private properties on three sides and a public street to the south.

1. Place a 30 ft by 40 ft (9 m by 12 m) viewing platform within the property lines. Regrade the site to create a level area for the viewing platform. Indicate the finish elevation of the platform. The finish elevation must be 6 in (0.15 m) above the level area.

2. Regrade the site so that water will flow around and away from the viewing platform. The slope of the regraded areas shall be at least 1% and no more than 20%. Contour lines within the property lines may be manipulated.

3. The existing trees and monument shall not be disturbed. Contour lines within tree drip lines shall not be disturbed.

4. Changes in contour lines that are not required for proper drainage should be avoided.

## Tips

- Use the sketch tools to draw the desired drainage lines and the minimum separation of contour lines.
- The *erase* tool affects all changes that have been made to a contour line. Undo affects the last action only.

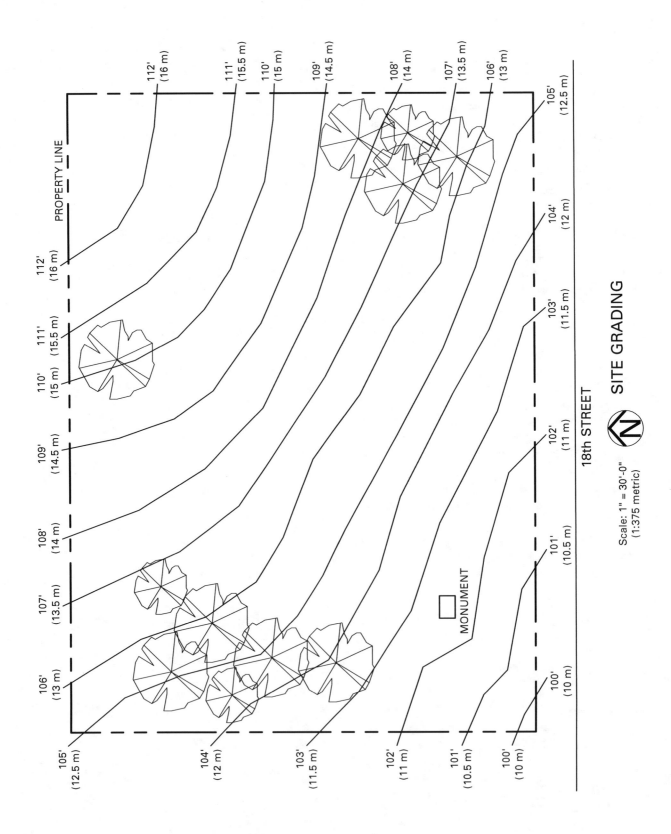

# PRACTICE EXAM: MULTIPLE CHOICE SOLUTIONS

| # | Answer | | # | Answer | | # | Answer |
|---|--------|---|---|--------|---|---|--------|
| 1. | B | | 26. | B | | 51. | B |
| 2. | A | | 27. | D | | 52. | A ■■■ D ■■ |
| 3. | C | | 28. | D | | 53. | C |
| 4. | A | | 29. | C | | 54. | **10%** |
| 5. | A ■ ■ D E ■ | | 30. | C | | 55. | A |
| 6. | C | | 31. | A | | 56. | D |
| 7. | C | | 32. | B | | 57. | D |
| 8. | B | | 33. | B | | 58. | **36,000 ft² (4000 m²)** |
| 9. | D | | 34. | A ■■■ D ■■ | | 59. | A ■■■ D ■■ |
| 10. | B | | 35. | B | | 60. | A |
| 11. | C | | 36. | D | | 61. | B |
| 12. | A | | 37. | C | | 62. | D |
| 13. | C | | 38. | A | | 63. | B |
| 14. | D | | 39. | D | | 64. | D |
| 15. | C | | 40. | C | | 65. | D |
| 16. | A | | 41. | D | | | |
| 17. | D | | 42. | C | | | |
| 18. | B | | 43. | D | | | |
| 19. | D | | 44. | B | | | |
| 20. | D | | 45. | A | | | |
| 21. | A ■ C D E ■ | | 46. | ■■■■ D E ■ | | | |
| 22. | C | | 47. | D | | | |
| 23. | C | | 48. | A | | | |
| 24. | D | | 49. | C | | | |
| 25. | A | | 50. | C | | | |

## 1. The answer is B.

Aligning the long axis of a rectangular building approximately 15° east of south provides the best overall balance between capturing heat during the lower morning temperatures and minimizing the intense west-facing solar radiation. The exact angle of the building east of south varies slightly depending on the climatic region, ranging from 25° for hot-humid climates to 5° for hot-arid climates, but averaging about 15°.

## 2. The answer is A.

When determining the required area for a leaching field, the architect should require a percolation test. A *percolation test* measures the amount of time it takes water in a test hole to drop 1 in (25). Based on this time, reference tables give the minimum length of piping, and therefore the ground area, that is required to handle a project's projected sewage flow volume.

A *potability* test evaluates drinking water for bacteria, pH, color, odor, turbidity, hardness, and other commonly found elements.

A *topographic survey* is not necessary if the proposed leaching field is relatively flat. It is important to determine where the water table is, but a high water table is generally revealed in the percolation test.

## 3. The answer is C.

A decreased runoff coefficient is not a consequence of inadequate water runoff control. The runoff coefficient is the fraction of total precipitation that is not absorbed into the ground. If there is not adequate control of water runoff, then the coefficient will increase, not decrease.

Accelerated soil creep, erosion of stream banks, and an increased load on the storm sewer system may all occur if there is inadequate runoff control.

## 4. The answer is A.

A *French drain*, sometimes called a subdrain, is a type of perimeter foundation subsurface drainage system. A continuous perforated pipe is placed near the footing of a foundation in a ditch lined with a filter fabric and filled with gravel. The drain collects water and directs it to daylight where it can drain to the ground or another appropriate collection point.

A *leader line* comes off a gutter, while a *strip drain* is a type of subdrain. A trench drain is a continuous drain placed at ground level and designed to catch runoff and divert it to a storm sewer, retention pond, or some other type of drainage collection system.

## 5. The answer is A, D, and E.

A *bioswale* is a shallow ditch lined with grass or other ground cover, and is designed to slow storm runoff and remove sediments and other contaminants while allowing the water to seep into the ground. An *infiltration basin* catches stormwater runoff and retains it until it can seep into the ground. *Pervious paving* allows stormwater to seep through the paving into the soil instead of running into storm sewers. All of these elements are sustainable approaches to reducing the amount of stormwater placed into storm sewers or natural waterways.

Catch basins, cisterns, and box culverts allow stormwater to run into the storm sewer system or off site.

## 6. The answer is C.

The best soil for slab-on-grade construction is poorly graded gravel (that is, gravel with uniform particle size). It has the highest bearing capacity of the four soil types listed and would provide drainage to minimize water infiltration.

The other options have lower bearing capacities. Any soil containing clay is problematic because of the possibility of expansion and the poor drainage quality of clays. Soils containing organic material should also be avoided for slab bearing. Soils are defined according to the standards of the Unified Soil Classification System.

## 7. The answer is C.

A 24 ft (7.3 m) road width is generally considered minimum for low to moderate speed roadways with two-way traffic, for both straight segments and curves. This same width is also considered a minimum for two-way driveways.

## 8. The answer is B.

The *heat island effect* is the tendency for architectural materials and paving to increase the temperature of their immediate environment. A paving material with a high albedo will reflect more of the sun's heat, thereby reducing the heat island effect.

*Albedo* is a measure of how much of the radiant energy that a surface receives is reflected rather than absorbed. It is expressed as a fraction from zero to one. A surface that reflects three-fourths of the energy it receives (and therefore absorbs the other one-fourth) has an albedo of 0.75.

Selecting a material with a low conductivity will not have as much of an effect on the site's temperature.

**9.    The answer is D.**

Option D includes three effective methods for minimizing noise to a building from an adjacent site. First, the building is placed as far away from the noise source as possible. Each doubling of the distance between a point source of noise and the receiver causes sound levels to drop by about six decibels. Next, a high, solid barrier is constructed as close to the noise source as possible. The effectiveness of a solid barrier increases as its height increases and as it is moved closer to the source. Finally, trees are used to attenuate the higher frequency sounds.

While the approaches shown in the other diagrams would help, none are as effective as option D. The ground cover shown in option A is a non-reflective surface but is only marginally effective in attenuating noise. The deeper row of trees shown in option B is good for attenuating high-frequency noise and the building is located at a distance from the noise source, but there is no solid barrier. In option C the building is located closer to the source and the barrier is not as high as in option D.

**10.    The answer is B.**

To maintain the continuity of the public space enclosure defined by the other buildings, an architect should be most sensitive to the *recess line*. In urban site planning, the recess line is the top of the full-width plane of a building facade, which effectively defines the enclosure of public space relative to the distance between it and an opposite facade. If there is any portion of the building above the recess line, it is set back to provide daylighting or views, so it does not affect the sense of enclosure of the public space. The building height and the recess line are not necessarily at the same elevation.

A *setback* is simply the minimum horizontal distance between the property line and the building. The *transition line* is a line running the full width of the facade and that may be expressed as a change of material or limited projection. The transition line may divide the facade somewhere below the recess line without altering the overall composition of the public space.

**11.    The answer is C.**

Building shapes that can focus or amplify blast energy should be avoided. This includes L-shaped and U-shaped buildings and buildings with reentrant corners or second-floor overhangs.

The other statements are true. Because a great deal of injury can be caused by flying glass, injury can be minimized by using laminated glass and by the proper design of glazing framing. Blast energy decreases exponentially with increased distance between the source of the blast and the building. Because of this, one of the most effective site planning strategies is to maximize the distance between the building and the outermost secured perimeter.

**12.    The answer is A.**

For a change in elevation of only 1 ft (305) in a distance of 300 ft (91 m), the slope of the house sewer can be easily decreased. However, the size of the sewer must be increased to maintain proper flow. As the slope of drainage pipe decreases the size must increase. The International Plumbing Code requires a minimum slope of $1/4$ in/ft (20 mm/m) for pipes with a diameter of $2\,1/2$ in (63.5) or less, $1/8$ in/ft (10 mm/m) for pipes from 3 in (76) to 6 in (152) in diameter, and $1/16$ in/ft (5 mm/m) for pipes with a diameter of 8 in (203) or larger. In this case, the pipe could be increased from 6 in (152) to 8 in (203) without much increase in cost because the cost of trenching, installation, and backfill would be the same.

Changing the angle of the house sewer to intercept the main line farther down the slope might be possible, but additional trenching would be more expensive than increasing the pipe size. In addition, option B is as poor choice because there is no information about the position or the slope of the main line. Changing the location of the building may not be possible due to setback requirements or other site planning decisions. Adding a manhole would not solve the problem of slope.

**13.    The answer is C.**

Because the contour lines in the middle of the section are at lower elevations and progress upward, section C-C represents a valley. Section A-A represents a uniform slope from elevation 10 up to elevation 14. Section B-B represents an upward slope from about elevation 6 to elevation 9. Section D-D represents a ridge.

## 14. The answer is D.

Zoning ordinances commonly regulate the maximum area of exterior signage to control the overall amount of signage in a given zone district. The International Building Code does have an appendix on signage, but this appendix is not mandatory unless specifically adopted by the local ordinance adopting the IBC. The IBC appendix primarily regulates signs' structural aspects, which may depend on the material and size. Restrictive covenants generally do not regulate signs except in residential areas. State laws do not regulate exterior building signage.

## 15. The answer is C.

24 ft (7.3 m) is the minimum recommended width for a two-way driveway coming off a street where vehicles may be turning into and out of the drive.

## 16. The answer is A.

The *Proctor test* determines the optimum compaction of site fill based on its density and optimum moisture content.

A *pit test* is simply a pit dug in the soil to allow visual inspection of the soil.

A *dry sample boring* is not a test but a method of extracting soil samples.

A *soil load* test determines the design load of soil by applying steadily increasing loads on a platform placed on the site.

## 17. The answer is D.

The FAR, or *floor area ratio*, is the total floor area of the building divided by the total site area. Based on the given building site, the total site area is 80,000 ft² (24 000 m²). The total floor area of the buildings in each option is 240,000 ft² (24 000 m²), so all options have a FAR of 3.0.

For sustainable design, the footprint of the building should be minimized to reduce disturbance of the natural landscaping and to minimize the impervious area. Although not part of the question, the parking, walks, grading, and other site development should also be minimized.

## 18. The answer is B.

In planning the location of a building on a site, the location of the sanitary sewer should be considered before the locations of the water main, underground telephone line, and power line. Because the sanitary sewer needs gravity flow to work properly and because the elevation of the sanitary sewer in the street is established, the location of the building may be determined by the maximum distance from the building to the existing street sewer that still results in the minimum required slope of the sewer line.

## 19. The answer is D.

A *stoop* design would make access difficult. It incorporates a first floor that is slightly elevated above the street to provide some privacy for the windows. Steps lead down to the street. Because the facade is typically located close to the frontage line, there is little room for ramps. The steps would create an inaccessible entry.

An *arcade* is a covered pedestrian way that overlaps the sidewalk. The sidewalk and storefronts are on the same level. A *forecourt* is a design where the building line is set back from the frontage line and a wall is placed at the frontage line, creating a semi-private courtyard. Although the wall creates a visual barrier, the sidewalk, forecourt, and building are on the same level. A *porch and fence* design separates the building and the sidewalk with a yard. A fence is placed at the frontage line with a porch placed in front of the building. With the porch and fence design, the sidewalk, access walk, porch, and building are typically placed on the same level.

## 20. The answer is D.

A 90° parking space configuration is the most efficient in terms of land use because the greatest number of spaces can be accommodated in any given length—approximately 11 cars in a 100 ft (30.5 m) length. The disadvantage of this parking configuration is that it is more difficult for the driver to maneuver within it, requiring the driver to make a 90° turn into or out of the parking space and to look out for traffic coming in both directions.

A 30° parking configuration is the least efficient, allowing only about 5 cars to park in a 100 ft (30.5 m) length.

## 21. The answer is A, C, and D.

To determine the regulations that pertain to a planned development around a wetlands area, the architect should investigate local and state governmental rules, and U.S. Army Corps of Engineers regulations.

Regulations for wetlands are established at the federal level and can be set by local and state governments. At the federal level the U.S. Army Corps of Engineers administers provisions of the Clean Water Act of 1972, which, among other things, regulates the discharge of dredged or fill material into United States waters, including wetlands. When wetlands do not fall under the jurisdiction of the Clean Water Act, as with isolated wetlands, then state and local governments may have established rules and regulations.

LEED credit may be earned for preserving portions of the site that are within 100 ft (30 m) of any wetland as defined by the U.S. Code of Federal Regulations, or of any isolated wetlands identified by state or local rule or within setback distances from wetlands prescribed in state or local regulations.

## 22.   The answer is C.

In an urban setting, a rear yard building would be most appropriate for a retail store.  In urban site planning, there are four basic types of site utilization based on where the building is located. With a *rear yard* type, the front of the building is placed on the lot line. Open space at the rear of the lot is used for parking, service, or other functions. This type is a good way for retail stores to expose a maximum amount of storefront to the street while defining an edge of an urban space.

A *courtyard* building occupies all or nearly all of the edges of a lot with a private interior courtyard. This building type is good where security or privacy is needed for the outdoor space. A *perimeter yard* building is located in the middle of the lot with open space surrounding it. It is often utilized in semi-urban or suburban locations for residential use or where a monumental appearance is desired. A *side yard* building occupies one side of the lot with the other side open. This configuration can be used to create a semiprivate yard or to orient the building for solar access.

## 23.   The answer is C.

The diagram shown in option C indicates a symmetrical layout on the site with the building visually connected with the plaza on a strong axis. Both of these are commonly used Baroque planning concepts, in which grand boulevards were used to connect palaces and other major buildings.

Although diagonal avenues were used in Baroque planning, the diagonal lines shown in option D are not strong enough to pick up the theme of diagonal avenues or boulevards.

## 24.   The answer is D.

According to ADA-ABA Accessibility Guidelines, the maximum slope of a curb cut, as with any ramp, is 1:12. The flared sides of the ramp may be sloped to a maximum of 1:10.

## 25.   The answer is A.

Eliminating parking lot lighting is a poor strategy for minimizing light pollution. Although eliminating any site lighting will reduce light pollution, some light is necessary for circulation and safety. For parking lots, light can be provided without spread onto adjacent properties or into the sky by using properly designed luminaires. The other options are all good strategies to minimize light pollution.

## 26.   The answer is B.

In order to determine the appropriate use for the slope, first calculate the grade according to the following formula.

$$G = \frac{d}{L} \times 100\%$$

$G$ is the grade measured as a percentage, $d$ is the vertical distance between points in feet (meters), and $L$ is the horizontal distance between points in feet (meters).

*In U.S. units:*

$$G = \frac{20 \text{ ft}}{250 \text{ ft}} \times 100\%$$
$$= 8\%$$

*In SI units:*

$$G = \frac{6 \text{ m}}{75 \text{ m}} \times 100\%$$
$$= 8\%$$

With an 8% grade, the site would best be used for buildings and walks. Parking should be planned for slopes from 1.5% to 5%. Slopes over 10% are difficult to walk on and building becomes more expensive. Slopes up to 25% should be landscaped to prevent erosion and slopes over 50% must be terraced to prevent erosion.

## 27.   The answer is D.

The fall equinox in the Northern Hemisphere is on or near September 22. On this day the days and nights are the same length and the sun rises and sets over the equator.

The sun is at its northernmost position on the summer solstice, about June 21, and at its southernmost position on the winter solstice, about December 21. The summer solstice is also when the days are longest in the Northern Hemisphere. The day or days when sunrise is earliest and sunset is latest can vary with location and do not always coincide precisely with the solstice.

The Northern and Southern Hemispheres experience opposite seasons, and in the Southern Hemisphere the fall equinox occurs on or about March 20, the winter solstice on or about June 21, and the summer solstice on or about December 21.

### 28.   The answer is D.

*Arterial streets* are public roads that connect freeways or expressways. A *local street* is a low capacity road that provides direct access to building sites and may be straight, curvilinear, a loop, or a cul-de-sac. A *collector street* connects local streets and arterial streets and is used for higher capacities than local streets. Collector streets empty into arterial streets. A service road, sometimes called a frontage road, is a local road that runs parallel to a freeway or expressway and that provides access to the property bordering it.

### 29.   The answer is C.

The *probable maximum flood* (PMF) is the most severe flood that may reasonably be possible for a particular location. It results from a combination of the most critical meteorological and hydrological conditions in a drainage basin. The water level in this type of flood is higher than in a standard projected flood. PMFs are used for designing facilities and structures that must be subject to almost no risk of flooding.

A *standard projected flood* (SPF) is a flood that may be expected from the most severe combination of meteorological and hydrological conditions in a particular location, excluding extremely rare combinations as with a PMF. SPFs are typically expressed as a probability frequency, such as a 50-year flood, which means that there is a 2% probability in any one year that a flood would occur.

The National Flood Insurance Program (NFIP) standards require that local participating governments adopt minimum floodplain management plans. These plans include requirements for zoning, subdivision of buildings, and special-purpose floodplain ordinances. These requirements must be met in order for federal flood insurance to be available for property owners. The floodplain defined by the NFIP may not be as high as the PMF. Local flood regulations may be more or less strict than the NFIP requirements, but typically do not define a floodplain as high as the PMF.

### 30.   The answer is C.

The maximum allowable cross slope for a sidewalk is 2%. This allows for drainage to prevent water ponding and freezing, but the sidewalk remains usable by people with disabilities. A sidewalk with a slope of more than 2% is difficult for wheelchair users to travel along.

### 31.   The answer is A.

*Battering* is the sloping or recessing of successive courses of stone or masonry to help resist soil thrust and overturning.

### 32.   The answer is B.

The basic allowable height and floor area of a building is based on the construction type and the occupancy group. The floor area can be increased if an automatic sprinkler system is installed and if a prescribed minimum open space is maintained between the building and adjacent buildings or property lines. (The open space prevents fire from spreading from one building to another and allows emergency vehicle access.) The exact formula for determining the allowable increase in floor area varies depending on which code is being used, but the concept is similar for all codes.

Once the construction type is established and the distance from the building to property lines is known, the codes establish the required hourly fire protection of exterior walls and the required fire protection rating of openings. Reducing the allowable height of a building has no effect on the allowable area of the building.

### 33.   The answer is B.

Of the options listed, simply placing bars on windows would be the least effective crime prevention technique, according to the principles of *crime prevention through environmental design* (CPTED). CPTED is the process of designing security into architecture. The various strategies it uses are implemented through architectural design, electronic methods, and organizational methods. Architectural design methods include the use of defensible space concepts that deny admission to a target and create a perception that there is a risk in selecting a target; such concepts include natural access control, natural surveillance, territorial reinforcement, and legitimate activity support. Mechanical access control including locks and window bars supplement natural and electronic access-control measures. Natural access control elements include fences, hedges, and gates, which create the perception that selecting the target is a risk. Electronic methods include the use of locks, alarms, access control, electronic surveillance, and similar techniques. Organizational methods include the use of human resources such as guards, door attendants, receptionists, and the like.

**34.    The answer is B, C, E, and F.**

A site survey provided by a surveyor should include the location and width of easements, land contours, position of existing roads adjacent to the site, and location of existing buildings on the site. Other features that are commonly found on a site survey include the legal boundaries of the site, utility lines adjacent to the site or that cross through the site, the location of benchmarks, and structures near the boundaries of the site.

The survey typically does not include suggested view planes. A view plane is an imaginary plane established from one point on a site out toward other points at given distances, elevations, and angles from the starting point. A view plane defines an area above which structures on adjacent sites cannot be built. The purpose of a view plane is to preserve views from a site, and it is typically established by a local governmental jurisdiction. Although a site survey should show the location and type of existing utilities on and adjacent to the site, the surveyor is not responsible for suggesting which ones may need to be removed.

**35.    The answer is B.**

ADA-ABA Accessibility Guidelines require that accessible parking and loading areas be nearly level, allowing only enough slope for drainage. This is to make it easy to enter or leave a vehicle. The allowable slope is 2% or approximately 1:48.

**36.    The answer is D.**

Zoning regulations define the minimum setback distances from the property line to the building. Building codes allow for increases in the maximum building area depending on the available open space around a building, which may in some cases suggest a setback greater than the minimum. Bulk planes are affected by the setback distance but more often restrict the overall height of a building and how upper stories set back from a given starting point. Fire zone requirements generally determine the allowable construction type and minimum access for firefighting equipment.

**37.    The answer is C.**

Though municipal utility maps and the civil engineer may have information about the location of utility lines, an architect's primary source of such information is the utility companies, which maintain accurate and complete maps and other information regarding the services they provide. The electrical engineer would use utility location information gathered by the site survey or the architect, and would request additional technical information on power availability and the like from the utility company.

**38.    The answer is A.**

All the strategies listed will gain new construction project LEED points except reducing construction activity pollution. This does not gain points but is a prerequisite for applying for LEED credits.

**39.    The answer is D.**

*Blackwater* is wastewater that contains toilet or urinal waste. Storm sewers may not carry this type of waste.

Sanitary sewers carry blackwater. A building sewer is that portion of the sanitary sewer system from 3 ft (915) beyond the building connecting to the public sewers or to a private sewage disposal system. A house sewer (sometimes also called the house drain) is that portion of the sanitary sewer system within the building and to a point 3 ft (915) outside the building. Both of these components of a building sewer system would carry blackwater.

**40.    The answer is C.**

An exterior pedestrian walk must be accessible, so the design solution must include a ramp. Options A and B do not include a ramp, and so are not viable options. Either of options C or D would work, but of the two, option C is the better design solution. A single ramp for such a short distance would work for all people and be safer. Further, if the ramp is 14 ft (4267) long, the slope is less than the maximum 1:12, which is generally recommended. For option D, it would also be difficult to locate the beginning and end of the ramp at the recommended location near the bottom and top of the steps.

Option A is incorrect not only because it does not include a ramp, but also because it has only two steps, which is dangerous. There should be a minimum of three steps in a flight of stairs.

**41.    The answer is D.**

An *edge* is a linear element other than a path that forms a boundary between two districts or that breaks some type of continuity. A solid wall of a building (even if penetrated by doors and windows) aligned with other buildings on the same street would form an edge. In this situation, the edge of the building would break the continuity of the street and open space. It would not be a *path* because it cannot be traveled on. A *district* is a two-dimensional area and a *node* is a strategic center of interest that people can enter.

**42.  The answer is C.**

Local ordinances typically establish *view plane restrictions* to protect scenic views from a specific point or area. Buildings cannot be built that obstruct these views. This is only possible through local control rather than through building codes or easements. Although zoning restrictions limit the height and bulk of buildings, they do so based on individual lot restrictions rather than with imaginary lines drawn through a site, or several sites, from some point.

**43.  The answer is D.**

Of the options listed, video surveillance monitored by a central station would be the best electronic security system to protect the exterior of an office building. Audio alarms would not be appropriate to protect the exterior of a building because of possible false alarms caused by on- and off-site noises. Motion sensors would not be useful because of possible false alarms caused by animals, air turbulence, and other interferences. Thermal detectors are only useful in relatively small rooms and are used to detect torches and other high-heat sources.

**44.  The answer is B.**

Planting strips for trees should be a minimum of 6 ft (1830), though some sources recommend a minimum of 7 ft (2130). Planting strips for grass should be a minimum of 4 ft (1220).

**45.  The answer is A.**

An *egress court*, which is a type of exit discharge, is not required to make a site accessible for egress. An egress court is a court or yard on private property that provides access to a public way from one or more exits. When access to a public way cannot be provided, the International Building Code allows an exception to provide dispersal areas if they are at least 50 ft (15 240) away from the building, on the same lot, and provide at least 5 ft² (0.28 m²) for each person. These requirements are building code egress mandates, and are not required by ADA-ABA Accessibility Guidelines.

Abrupt vertical changes in level cannot exceed ¹/₄ in (6) as with all accessible routes. An accessible route such as a sidewalk cannot have a slope greater than 1:20 (5%) unless it is treated as a ramp and is in compliance with all ramp

requirements, including handrails, curbs, and requirements for maximum rise and length. Cross slopes may be up to 1:50 (2%) for drainage.

**46.  The answer is A, B, C, and F.**

The site design elements that influence fire protection and are the responsibility of the architect include the position and size of building canopies, surface material outside of the building, traffic control fences and bollard positions, and the width of fire apparatus access drives. While the local fire department may have suggestions or requirements for these features, the exact design is the responsibility of the architect.

The position of fire hydrants on streets and the size and position of other utility elements are the responsibility of the various municipal utilities.

**47.  The answer is D.**

A storage shed or other permanent structure cannot be built over a utility easement. Generally, nothing except sidewalks, driveways, and landscaping can be placed over a utility easement. In some cases, parking lots may be built over easements, but local regulations should be consulted.

**48.  The answer is A.**

According to the Secretary of the Interior's Standards for Rehabilitation, repairing an existing exterior cornice molding could be done to a historic property undergoing rehabilitation treatment. The Standards for Rehabilitation emphasize the retention and repair of historic materials but give some latitude for replacing damaged elements. Repairing a damaged or deteriorated historic element, rather than replacing it, is allowed.

Removing historic materials or altering internal spaces should be avoided. Chemical or physical treatments that could damage historic materials must not be used. If changes that have been made to the original structure also have historic significance, they must be retained and preserved.

**49.  The answer is C.**

In a residential subdivision, designing stairways within solid structures would be counter to reducing the potential for criminal activity. According to the principles of crime prevention through environmental design (CPTED), stairways and elevators should be located within view of other areas.

Using low plantings or post-and-rail fences helps to define private areas and gives a sense of territorial reinforcement. Locating entry doors and common areas within view of the street or other neighbors provides natural surveillance.

**50.  The answer is C.**

There are 43,560 ft² in one acre (about the size of a football field) and 10,000 m² in one hectare.

**51.  The answer is B.**

The size of the lot is the most important factor in determining if it is feasible to use a ground source heat pump. Ground source heat pumps require long lengths of pipe buried in the ground. Roughly 400 ft to 600 ft (120 m to 183 m) of pipe are required for each 12,000 Btu/hr (3500 W) of heating or cooling capacity. Although they may be buried vertically, it is more cost efficient to bury them horizontally. Therefore, the available size of the lot would be an early indication of whether this heating method will be feasible.

Ground temperature is important to know but it would affect only the exact length of pipe required and the depth of pipe.

**52.  The answer is B, C, E, and F.**

During preliminary site planning, minimizing the building footprint is an effective sustainability strategy. It reduces the amount of site disturbance and provides more area for landscaping and porous paving, both of which reduce runoff. Positioning buildings along contours minimizes the amount of earthwork and site clearing required. Locating buildings and parking areas near roads minimizes the amount of paving required for access roads. An infiltration basin catches stormwater runoff and retains it until it can seep into the ground. This would reduce the amount of stormwater added to the storm sewer system and avoid possible contamination of natural water courses.

A *greenfield site* is undeveloped land that may contain existing vegetation and native ecosystems. A better sustainable strategy is to remediate a brownfield site, which is previously developed land that may contain contaminated soil. Providing maximum lawn area is not a good strategy because lawns require significant amounts of water and maintenance.

**53.  The answer is C.**

For a hot-arid climate, a building's thermal mass should be maximized, not minimized. (Minimizing the thermal mass is a good strategy in a hot-humid climate.) All the other design strategies are good ways to mitigate the effects of a hot-arid climate on comfort.

**54.  The answer is 10%.**

To determine the slope, use the following formula.

$$G = \frac{d}{L} \times 100\%$$

G is the grade measured as a percentage, d is the vertical distance between points in feet (meters), and L is the horizontal distance between points in feet (meters).

*In U.S. units:*

$$G = \frac{30 \text{ ft}}{300 \text{ ft}} \times 100\%$$
$$= 10\%$$

*In SI units:*

$$G = \frac{9 \text{ m}}{90 \text{ m}} \times 100\%$$
$$= 10\%$$

**55.  The answer is A.**

The most important characteristic of an on-site road designed to serve parking areas and service vehicles is the slope. An on-site road should be laid out to avoid steep slopes, which may be difficult to drive on, especially when the surface is icy. A *tangent* is the straight portion of a road connected to the curved portions. *Horizontal alignment* is the road layout in the horizontal direction and *vertical alignment* is the layout in the vertical direction. While all are important in the design of roads for higher speed traffic, slope is the most critical for slow speed service use such as parking and service roads.

**56.  The answer is D.**

The first zoning ordinance in the United States was passed in 1916 in New York City. Although San Francisco and Los Angeles enacted ordinances to limit the location of obnoxious uses and to define how undeveloped land could be used, New York City enacted the first comprehensive zoning ordinance in 1916. The ordinance established height and setback controls and bulk planes, and separated incompatible uses to prevent the encroachment of industry into Manhattan's office and department store district. In 1926 the United States Supreme Court upheld the right of a city to enact zoning ordinances.

**57.    The answer is D.**

When a building design exceeds the maximum height allowance and the building height cannot be reduced, the owner should apply for a variance. A *variance* is an allowed deviation from zoning regulations. They are often granted where it is impossible or difficult to meet a zoning requirement or where a zoning ordinance does not completely cover unusual conditions.

A *conditional use permit* is given by a city or zoning jurisdiction to allow, if certain conditions are met, an otherwise prohibited use. This would not be appropriate for a situation where the allowed building height was exceeded.

An *easement* is the right to use a portion of land owned by another for a specific purpose.

A *PUD*, or planned unit development, is a planning tool for large tracts of land that gives a developer discretion in how the land is developed. Aspects of the plan must comply with standards and restrictions determined by the local planning agency.

**58.    The answer is 36,000 ft² (4000 m²).**

The maximum allowable buildable area is the area of the lot multiplied by the FAR, or floor area ratio. In this case the total area of the site is

$$A = wd$$

The floor area ratio is 2.0, so the buildable area is

$$A_{buildable} = w(\text{FAR})$$

*In U.S. units:*

$$A = wd = (120 \text{ ft})(150 \text{ ft}) = 18,000 \text{ ft}^2$$

$$A_{buildable} = A(\text{FAR}) = (18,000 \text{ ft}^2)(2.0) = 36,000 \text{ ft}^2$$

*In SI units:*

$$A = wd = (40 \text{ m})(50 \text{ m}) = 2000 \text{ m}^2$$

$$A_{buildable} = A(\text{FAR}) = (2000 \text{ m}^2)(2.0) = 4000 \text{ m}^2$$

The area within the setbacks has nothing to do with the maximum allowable building area. However, it would influence the number of stories of the building.

**59.    The answer is B, C, E, and F.**

Hydrostatic water problems are those that occur when water at the foundation is under pressure. To address hydrostatic water problems near a basement foundation, an architect should consider using geotextiles, gravel fill below the floor slab, positive slope away from the building, and sump pumps. These would be in addition to the standard design elements such as using an appropriate waterproofing membrane and a foundation drain. Geotextiles and gravel fill use air space to interrupt the pressure between the water and the foundation or slab. A positive slope helps keep water away from the foundation. Sump pumps remove any water that may penetrate the structure.

Dampproofing would not be appropriate if hydrostatic pressure may be present because dampproofing is not designed to stop water under pressure. Pervious paving would allow water to seep into the soil around the foundation, exacerbating the problem.

**60.    The answer is A.**

An *earthwork diagram* is used to show approximately how much of a building site needs to be regraded. It is sometimes called a cut-and-fill diagram. In order to minimize construction costs, the areas of cut should approximately equal the areas that require fill so that earth does not have to be imported or hauled off the site. Using the area of each portion of the diagram and the vertical distance between contours, the volume of earth that has to be moved can be calculated fairly accurately.

**61.    The answer is B.**

Each option listed has its own disadvantages. However, a brownfield would probably be the most buildable because, although it would take additional money and time, contaminates could be removed or otherwise mitigated. In addition, federal tax credits and incentive programs may be available to encourage the use of a brownfield site.

A floodplain would be very difficult to build on, assuming that the local, state, and federal regulations allowed it at all, because increased construction costs and continuing insurance costs could make it economically infeasible. Wetlands and endangered species habitats could not be used for development.

**62.    The answer is D.**

A material with a low albedo and a low conductivity such as dark wood would be most comfortable and moderate the microclimate best. Brick, concrete, and stone have higher albedos and would make the surrounding area hotter in the summer. Their high conductivity would also make them feel hot to the touch. Planting grass around the pavers will improve the albedo of a brick deck slightly, but dark wood still has a lower albedo. Also, wood has the lowest conductivity of the materials listed and would feel less hot in the summer.

**63.    The answer is B.**

Layout B sets the parking spaces perpendicular to the row of shops, making it easy for people to park relatively close to the stores they want and to reach the mall without walking through parked cars. The driveway locations and access aisle also allow for fire department access to the shops and easy pickup and dropoff.

Layout A forces people to walk through parked cars to get to the shops and creates conflict between circulation traffic and cars entering and exiting the row of spaces near the mall. Layout C concentrates incoming and outgoing traffic into one driveway, forces people to cross through parked cars, and doesn't provide easy building access for fire department and other emergency services. Although layout D distributes incoming and outgoing traffic from the street and sets parking spaces perpendicular to the row of shops, it forces emergency vehicles to travel through the parking area.

**64.    The answer is D.**

Under the revised ADA-ABA Accessibility Guidelines, the minimum width of a van parking space is 132 in (3350) while the minimum width for a car parking space is 96 in (2440). Each accessible parking space also requires an access aisle at least 60 in (1525) wide that runs alongside the full length of the parking space.

**65.    The answer is D.**

A *silt fence* is a temporary construction designed to filter water runoff from a construction site and trap sediment before it is washed into drains or nearby bodies of water.

A *bioswale* is a shallow ditch lined with grass or other ground cover. Like a silt fence, it is designed to slow storm runoff and remove sediments, but it is a permanent construction. *Riprap* is rock along a watercourse or drainage area designed to prevent erosion. *Screen grating* would not prevent sediment runoff.

# PRACTICE EXAM: VIGNETTE SOLUTIONS

## SITE DESIGN: PASSING SOLUTION

This vignette requires that the examinee plan the layout of two buildings, an outdoor space, and vehicular and pedestrian circulation on a given site to satisfy program constraints and the influences of site features and legal requirements.

**Solving Approach**

Step 1  Because the café/bookstore entrance must have noonday sun, it should face directly south. Because it must have a view of the lake, the block for the café/bookstore can be oriented and placed in the northwest portion of the site in such a way that trees are disturbed as little as possible. Allow enough space on the north for the service drive.

Step 2  The apartment block must be near the café/bookstore, and its entrance must connect to the plaza. This suggests that the apartment entrance should be oriented to the north or the east and placed in the southwest portion of the site. Locate the apartment building so that its height does not block the noonday sun on the entrance to the café/bookstore. The apartment is located so that it blocks the plaza from the wind.

Step 3  With the buildings and plaza placed on the western portion of the site, the parking will have to be placed on the east portion. Draw a simple rectangular block of parking with a central aisle. This is the most efficient, as well as the easiest to move around or rotate if necessary. Place the accessible parking spaces as close to the apartment entrance as possible.

Step 4  With the service entrance on the north side of the café/bookstore, draw a service drive from the service entrance east to 13th Avenue. This is the most direct connection and avoids going through any parking area.

Step 5  Because only one curb cut is allowed, the access to the parking area must be from the drive drawn in step 4. Locate the parking area near the buildings to meet the maximum distance requirements for the accessible parking spaces. This, in turn, suggests that another drive must be placed to connect the southern portion of the parking area to the drive completed in step 4.

Step 6  Draw the pedestrian plaza so that it meets the area requirements and has a view of the lake. Move and/or rotate the apartment building so that it is close to the required accessible parking and so that its entrance connects to the plaza.

Step 7  Check for disturbed trees and other required minimum or maximum distances.

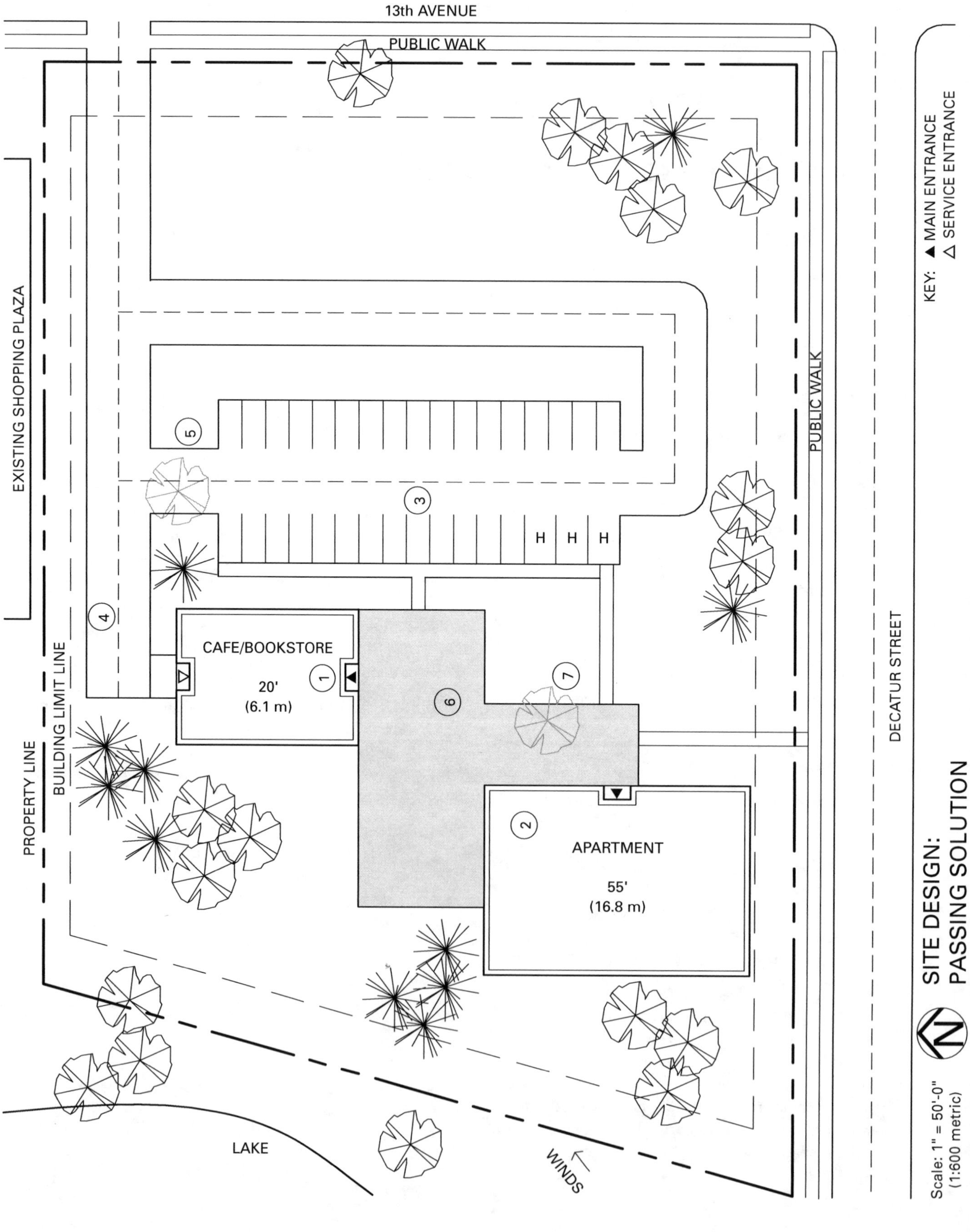

13th AVENUE

PUBLIC WALK

EXISTING SHOPPING PLAZA

PROPERTY LINE

BUILDING LIMIT LINE

⑤

③

H H H

④

CAFE/BOOKSTORE

20'
(6.1 m)

①

⑥

⑦

②

APARTMENT

55'
(16.8 m)

PUBLIC WALK

DECATUR STREET

LAKE

WINDS

N

KEY: ▲ MAIN ENTRANCE
△ SERVICE ENTRANCE

SITE DESIGN:
PASSING SOLUTION

Scale: 1" = 50'-0"
(1:600 metric)

# SITE DESIGN:
# FAILING SOLUTION

## Pitfalls

Note 1 The main entry to the café/bookstore is on the north, so it does not receive noonday sun.

Note 2 The plaza is undersized by about 900 ft² (84 m²). The program will allow some variation, about 10%, so the plaza may not be more than about 700 ft² (65 m²) below the given size.

Note 3 The plaza has only a limited view of the lake.

Note 4 Eight trees have been disturbed, two more than allowed by the program.

Note 5 There is no connection between the walkway system and the public sidewalk.

Note 6 Although planting has been added to the southern portion of the plaza (to protect against winds and to shield the service entrance on the east), there is no planting on the west side of the service entrance.

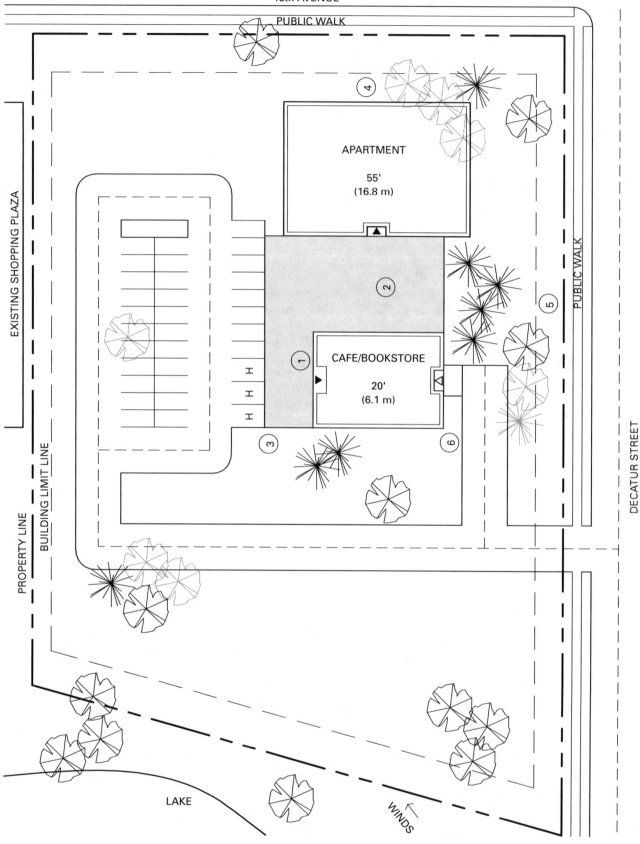

13th AVENUE

PUBLIC WALK

APARTMENT

55'
(16.8 m)

④

②

①

CAFE/BOOKSTORE

20'
(6.1 m)

③

⑥

⑤

EXISTING SHOPPING PLAZA

PROPERTY LINE

BUILDING LIMIT LINE

PUBLIC WALK

DECATUR STREET

LAKE

WINDS

KEY:  ▲ MAIN ENTRANCE
      △ SERVICE ENTRANCE

SITE DESIGN:
FAILING SOLUTION

N

Scale: 1" = 50'-0"
(1:600 metric)

# SITE GRADING: PASSING SOLUTION

This vignette requires the examinee to place an object of a given size within a site and readjust existing contour lines to control water flow while conforming to specific site requirements.

## Solving Approach

Step 1 Begin by estimating the most likely place for the viewing platform. In this case, the examinee decided to orient the platform with its longer dimension parallel to the property lines instead of to the contour lines; the latter is often easier, but either way can work here. Because the contour lines run diagonally across the site, the first high contour line that forms the level area is best located near the northeast corner of the platform.

Step 2 Begin with the high point of that portion of the site that needs to be regraded. Because contour 110 (15 m) runs under the drip line of a tree, contour 109 (14.5 m) is the highest contour that can be easily and flexibly changed, and this makes it a good place to start. Leave space below it for manipulating other contour lines. Begin to create a swale here that will divert water away from the platform. Remember that the contour lines of swales, or valleys, "point" uphill. The contour line that is manipulated to start the swale (that is, the highest contour line to be changed) will loop around the object on its downhill side to create the level area on which the object sits.

Step 3 Progressing downhill, continue forming swales with the contour lines so that water from higher areas is kept from flowing onto the platform. If this proves difficult, the initial contour line that forms the level area for the built object may need to be moved uphill or downhill.

Step 4 When changing contour lines, do not disturb contours where they cross existing objects or pass within the drip lines of trees. In this example, contours through the monument cannot be disturbed.

Step 5 Verify that no two contour lines are close enough together to form a slope greater than 20% or far enough apart to form a slope less than 1%. In this case, with 1 ft (0.5 m) contour lines, no two contour lines can be closer together than 5 ft (2.5 m) or farther apart than 100 ft (50 m).

Step 6 Mark the elevation of the viewing platform 6 in (0.15 m) above the flat graded area.

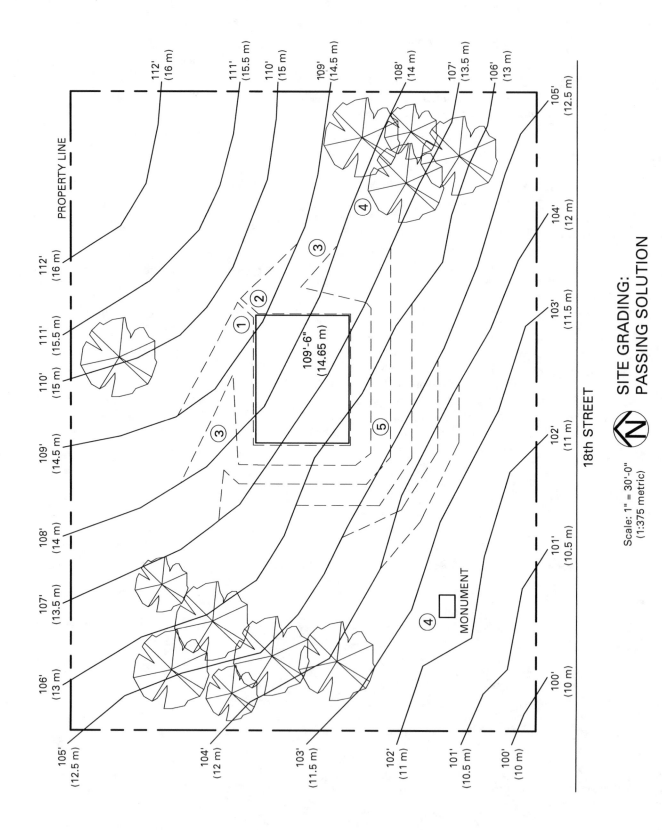

SITE GRADING:
PASSING SOLUTION

Scale: 1" = 30'-0"
(1:375 metric)

## SITE GRADING: FAILING SOLUTION

### Pitfalls

Note 1 The graded area for the platform is not level. It slopes from contour 107 (13.5 m) up to contour 108 (14 m).

Note 2 Contours 105, 106, and 107 (12.5 m, 13 m, and 13.5 m) are too close, resulting in a slope exceeding 20%.

Note 3 Water is diverted onto the northeast side of the platform. There is a 108 ft (14 m) grade directly next to the 107 ft 6 in (13.65 m) elevation of the pad.

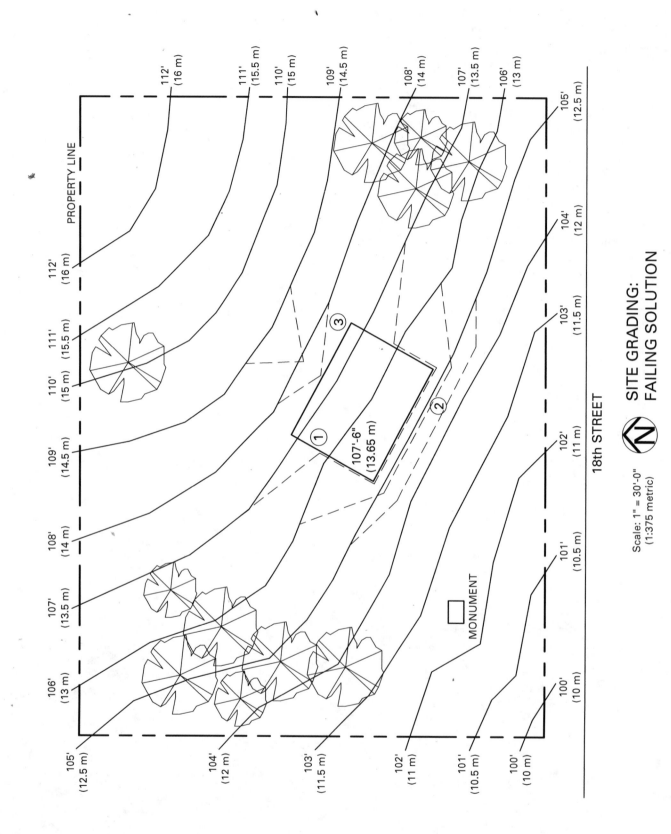

SITE GRADING:
FAILING SOLUTION

Scale: 1" = 30'-0"
(1:375 metric)